SING A
GENTLE BREEZE

SING A GENTLE BREEZE

The Story of a
Disintegrating Family
Seeking Wholeness

Mary Soergel

TYNDALE HOUSE PUBLISHERS, INC.
Wheaton, Illinois
COVERDALE HOUSE PUBLISHERS, LTD.
Eastbourne, England

Library of Congress Catalog Card Number 76-47301. ISBN 0-8423-5889-7, paper. Copyright © 1977 by Tyndale House Publishers, Inc., Wheaton, Illinois. All rights reserved. First printing, February 1977. Printed in the United States of America.

Dedicated, in love,
to Karen and Jack Swanson

ACKNOWLEDGMENTS

The author wishes to acknowledge her gratitude to the following people whose ministries have profoundly affected the course of the story told in this book: Reverend Charles Lowder, Reverend Gene Lavine, Father Bob Bales, Reverend Edwin Ziemann, Father Dick Korzinek, Reverend Ferd Bahr, Reverend Nate Thorpe, and Willa Dorsey.

My thanks to Dr. John Crawford for his consistent concern for Scott and his family down through the years, and for permission to use some of his letters.

To Ed and Esther Wessling for sharing their lives so openly, for the insight gained, we owe deep gratitude.

For all the people whose prayers have supported us through the years, especially the Saturday morning prayer group of the First Congregational Church, Oconomowoc, Wis., the Living Waters Fellowship and St. Jerome's Church of Oconomowoc, and the Women's Aglow Board, Milwaukee, Wis., I ask God's blessing.

Most of all, I want to thank my husband and my children for allowing me the freedom to tell the truth.

CONTENTS

CHAPTER ONE

MIRACLES

Mary backed out of the parking space in front of the doctor's office. The slim boy on the seat beside her leaned his head back, closing his eyes. Turning onto the highway, she squealed the tires—as if the unaccustomed speed would signal her frustrations to someone who could help her.

Her mind rebelled. "I know there's something really wrong with Scott. Why couldn't I make the doctor realize it too?"

Questions were still chasing around in her mind that evening as she stood at the kitchen sink doing the supper dishes. "Why is Scott so tired all the time? Why did he leave the table to go lie down when he hadn't finished eating? Why doesn't he practice his tuba anymore? Why doesn't he work on his Scout badges like he used to? Why is his schoolwork slipping so fast? His teacher even called him in to say he'd be kicked out of the honor society if he didn't shape up."

"Mother, come here quick!" The urgency in Josh's voice drew her, running, into the living room where the children had been playing the piano and dancing around.

Scott lay at the foot of the stairs. His arms and legs jerked in short, quick spasms. His back arched. His eyes were opened wide, the pupils almost hidden beneath the upper eyelids. The whites of his eyes bulged outward, pink veins glowing.

Josh, Gretchen, Heidi, and Becca seemed like statues,

frozen to the floor as they stared at their brother. Scott's movements slowed until the shirt that had been moving rapidly up and down seemed to tuck itself around the quiet chest, lying completely still. His eyes were now closed.

Mary knelt, put her head against Scott's chest, felt for the wrist with searching fingers. "His pulse is all right. It's fast, but it feels strong. He's breathing. Josh, get a blanket. Cover him up."

She ran for the phone in the kitchen and with stabbing fingers dialed the doctor's number. She heard the phone ring on, feeling it was calling out to an empty house.

"I'm sorry, Dr. Schumann is out of town." It was the voice of the answering service. "Dr. Newmann is taking his calls."

"Please, God, let him be home," she whispered as she dialed. The calm voice that answered said he would be right out.

She dropped an ounce of fear as she ran back to kneel by the blanket-covered body, feeling again for the slender wrist. More unanswered questions. The sharp barking of the dog signaled the doctor's arrival.

As if in response, Scott's eyes opened. They focused on his mother's face as Josh opened the front door. The doctor came in and knelt beside Scott.

"Don't look so worried, Mother," Scott's steady voice said reassuringly. "I just fell down a few steps. I'm all right."

The doctor looked up at Mary, a frown wrinkling his forehead. He reached in his bag and pulled out a flash-light. Scott's steady breathing was the only sound in the room as the flashlight blinked off and on in front of his eyes. The doctor pulled up Scott's shirt and placed his stethoscope against his chest. He closed his eyes as his fingers thumped the boy's back, moving the stethoscope around. He knelt in silence for a moment, his eyes on

Scott's face. The boy's eyes were clear, his expression alert.

With an inscrutable look on his face, the doctor stood up, took his coat from the chair where he had thrown it, and clicked his bag shut. "Didn't you tell me on the phone that Dr. Schumann saw Scott this morning and said there was nothing wrong with him?"

Mary nodded dumbly.

"Well, I don't think there's anything wrong with him either. Put him to bed and see that he gets a good night's rest."

Mary shook her head as the door slammed, as if to shake out the feeling of disapproval the doctor had left behind him. She looked at the three little girls who were sitting on the bottom step. Their eyes, an almost identical shade of dark brown, were fastened on her face.

She tried to smile reassuringly. "I'm sure he's going to be all right, girls. You'd better go up and get ready for bed. Gretch, will you please tuck Becca in tonight?"

"Come on, Becca, I'll read you a story. Do you want to hear about Piglet or Pooh Bear?" The chubby hand reached out for the small one. Heidi followed them up the stairs. Mary looked at Josh, a year and a half younger than Scott, but already almost six inches taller. His brown eyes were filled with fear.

"I don't think there's anything to be excited about, Josh, but I think he'd better sleep down here tonight. I don't want to take a chance that he might get up and fall down the stairs again. I'll go up and get ready for bed. Why don't you move the twin bed mattresses down here? I'll sleep on the floor with him. I'll call Ben Schumann the first thing in the morning."

During the long hours of the sleepless night Scott's symptoms flew around in his mother's head, tracing a vapor trail too wispy to put in any proper sequence. As the hands of the clock moved toward midnight, Scott became more and more agitated, the quiet periods shorter in duration, less frequent. His body writhed from side to side, his arms poked out as at an invisible assailant. He sat up on the mattress, eyes staring wildly about him, seeming to see nothing at all. He clutched his head between his hands, rocking back and forth. "Oh, my head, my head."

"Scott, what's wrong? Does your head hurt?" Mary rolled off the mattress, crawled quickly across the small space between them, and put her hands on Scott's shoulders, shaking him softly. "Scott, wake up, wake up."

Slowly his hands dropped from his head. He blinked his eyes and looked at his mother. The corners of his mouth formed a sweet smile. "Oh, hi, Mom."

Even as he said the words, the smile faded. He dropped on his back in instant sleep. As if they were a cast of two rehearsing before an exacting director, the scene was repeated over and over, the lines and actions varying only slightly until the first rays of light shone across the fields and into the living room windows.

"Oh, Mother, look at the sunrise. Look at the color of that sky. Isn't it beautiful?" Instead of the frantic look, Scott's eyes seemed to be glowing, reflecting the early morning light. He looked around the room. "What are we doing down here?"

"Oh, you were having trouble sleeping, so Josh moved the mattresses down for us."

"That was nice." His eyelids closed, his breathing became slow and even. He slept peacefully. Mary lay watching as the shadows of the rising sun cast longer lines on the face so strangely young for his fourteen years. Realizing that sleep was impossible, she got up and walked into the kitchen. While the coffee was bubbling, she sat at the kitchen table, pencil in hand, writing down every single thing she could think of that had any relationship to this frightening condition. Her mind ferreted back through the years she had spent in nursing school, trying to dig up any helpful pieces of information. She waited impatiently until the hands of the clock said seven, then picked up the phone.

"Ben, I'm sorry to call you so early. This is Mary. I'm really worried about Scott." She described the night to him, then read off the list she had written down.

With a tremendous feeling of relief, she heard him say, "I just don't know, Mary. Let's put him in the hospital and do some studies. Bring him up without any breakfast. I'll call and tell them he's on his way. Call me tomorrow at the office about eleven. I'll tell you what we've found. He'll probably have to stay in for just one night."

The next morning in the hospital Mary sat down on the edge of Scott's bed and tried to focus on his chatter. For the first time since she had known Ben Schumann, the doctor's voice had sounded evasive to her.

"Hi, Mary." Dr. Ben's brown eyes seemed to flick away from hers as he walked into the room and up to Scott's bed. "I'm going to talk with your mother a minute, Scott. You can get your things on and get ready to go home."

The doctor's reassuringly sturdy back moved ahead of her out into the hall and into an unoccupied room. He pointed at the chair against the wall. "Sit down."

He stood looking down at her for a moment. The twinkle in his eyes that she had seen so often when he told jokes at bridge parties was missing. Instead they held a look she had never seen before. Her intuition had been right. Something was seriously wrong with her son.

The situation began to feel unreal. Part of her mind seemed to escape her body, flying up to look down at the doctor in the white coat who stood talking to the woman in her red hat. She had put that hat on with what she had thought a bright display of courage. Now, to that part of her looking on, the hat was only ridiculous loops of yarn and silly sequins.

As if from a distance, she heard the doctor begin. "We have a problem. When I examined Scott yesterday, I noticed some changes in his eye grounds. The discs were choked. This can be evidence of intracranial pressure. I ordered a head film." The doctor paused.

Mary held her breath, as if by ceasing to breathe she could stop his voice.

"Mary, Scott has a brain tumor."

"Brain tumor." The vapor trail had followed her into the hospital. It seemed to write the words in large white letters above the doctor's head.

"The stomach symptoms were a red herring. There's nothing in his stomach symptoms to indicate a brain tumor. It's called a cranial pharyngioma. It's congenital. Scott was born with it; that's why we caught it on X ray. The oldest parts are calcified, opaque to X ray. It is a very unusual tumor. The only other one I've seen was on autopsy; this thirty-five-year-old guy had been having excruciating headaches. Nobody could discover the cause until he died and they cut his head open." He looked down at Mary, his eyes soft with concern. "Are you all right? Do you want me to get you something?"

"No. I'm fine." Mary was surprised at her calm voice. "What do we do now?"

"Get him into St. Luke's in Milwaukee. I know a good neurosurgeon. I'll see if he can get us a bed by tomorrow."

"Tomorrow?" Mary sounded shocked. "Can't he stay home until at least after Christmas? That's only a week away."

"No, Mary, he can't. Time can be very important. It would be too risky to wait. I'll call Dr. Levin right now. Check with the nurses' station before you go. I'll leave the message there for you."

Mary's knees felt too liquid to hold her weight. The doctor stood quietly waiting for her to get up out of her chair. He looked as if there was more he wanted to say. He opened his mouth, then closed it. His breath escaped softly through his teeth. His hand reached out to pat her cheek, then fell to her shoulder. He squeezed with a soft little shaking motion, turned abruptly, and walked from the room. Mary sat without moving as she heard his footsteps go down the hall.

"No, God, no." Mary whispered the words. She clenched her lips tightly together to keep her voice from exploding into a loud shout. She shook her head, stood up, and walked out the door.

Hours later, Mary paced up and down the sidewalk waiting for her husband's bus. She dabbed at her face with a big red bandana. Tears that wouldn't stop were cold on her cheeks. The blast of wind rounding the corner of the building stiffened the cloth that absorbed them.

Norman jumped off the bus as it rolled to a stop. Mary ran up to him. He put his arms around her and hugged her tightly. Her sobs came shuddering out unchecked. He let her cry for a moment, then shook her shoulders gently.

"OK, OK, knock it off. Come on, let's get home. I want to see Scott. Where are the car keys?"

She reached in her pocket. She felt only the frozen ball of bandana. "I must have lost them when I kept pulling out my hanky."

"Well, I have mine. We can get you some new ones." Norm started the engine and turned to his wife as he let the car warm up. "Does Scott know yet?"

"No." Mary shook her head. "I was afraid to tell him for fear I'd cry."

"OK. I'll tell him." Norm drove in silence for a moment.

"Mary." The tone was decisive. "I prayed all the way home on the bus. I got the feeling that Scott is going to be all right. So quit worrying." As the car stopped, Norman looked across at his wife and reached over to give her knee a reassuring squeeze. "You all right now?"

Mary nodded. Her lips formed some semblance of her usual smile. "I'm all right."

Mary stood at the kitchen sink, scrubbing at the breakfast, lunch, and dinner dishes. She tried not to listen to the murmur of voices that came to her from the living room.

"Please, Lord," her mind pleaded, "help Norm find the right words. And, Lord, help me at least not to cry."

She walked over to the refrigerator, where she could see through the pass-through into the living room. Norman was kneeling by the big armchair in the corner where Scott sat, his hand on the dog's head. She couldn't tell what they were saying. Their voices seemed an inaudible accompaniment to the background of music on the kitchen radio. She saw Scott nod his head, his hand patting Ebbie's head rather fast. As she watched, Norm squeezed Scott's knee, got up, and came out into the kitchen.

He leaned against the wall by the pass-through where Scott couldn't see him, looking across at his wife. She walked over to him as he shook his head, his brown eyes speaking more eloquently than words. He reached into his pocket for his bandana, blowing his nose hard. They stood, shoulders tight together, as they watched Scott give the dog's head a final pat. He got up from his chair and walked slowly up the stairs, dog at his heels, his hand pulling at the banister.

"What did he say?" Mary whispered.

"He said..." Norm hesitated and took a deep breath. "He said, 'OK, Dad, if that's what you say I should do, then that's what I'll do.' " Norm put his arms around his wife and rested his cheek against her hair, squeezing her tightly to him.

"I'll tell you what." Mary shook herself loose, her mind suddenly alive. "Let's have a special before-Christmas dinner tonight."

She walked to the foot of the stairs. "Josh, Gretchen, Heidi, Becca, where are you?" They came rushing down the stairs, pushing and shoving to stand closest to their mother.

"Scott has to go into Milwaukee to go to another hospital tomorrow, so we're going to have a special dinner for him tonight. What do you think we should have to eat?"

Mary's parents walked in the front door as the family was finishing dinner.

"Sit down, Grampy." Scott stood up, pulling out the chair. "You're just in time for a piece of pie. Guess what we had for dinner? Steak and French fries and garlic bread. You should have come a little earlier."

The bald man in the grey-striped suit picked up the fork on the plate that Mary put down in front of him. "Apple pie, my favorite."

"I'll just sit down over here. I'm rather tired." Mary's mother closed her eyes. The group at the table chattered their way through dessert as if nothing were different from any other evening.

"Let's all sing 'Silent Night.' Then I think I'm going to bed." Scott's voice sounded tired.

Grampy's rich baritone blended with the soprano of his grandchildren. The candles flickered as the family sang "sleep in heavenly peace." They watched Scott and his dog climb the stairs.

Mary rose quickly, starting to pick up the dishes. Her father picked up the ones he had used and followed her into the kitchen. "I think you're doing fine, just fine."

Mary blinked hard as the concern in her father's voice beckoned back the tears.

Her mother's voice came from the living room. "Come on, Malc. Let's go home. I'm very tired."

Mary held the door open for her parents.

"Let me know if there's anything we can do." Her father took his wife's arm protectively in his, helping her down the shallow step. Mary stood watching them as they walked slowly out to their car.

Later that night she woke within the circle of her husband's arms. She tried to recall the nightmare that had left her shuddering with fear, but realized as her mind became fully awake that she had not had a bad dream. She lay listening to Norman's quiet breathing.

"God," her mind spoke silently, "why can't I feel like Norm said he felt, sure that Scott will be all right? I thought I was the one with the most faith. Where did it go?"

The words seemed to slide off the ice inside her into the void around her. She got out of bed, picked up her robe, and knotted the belt tightly around her waist. As she walked down the stairs, she remembered the thumping sounds Scott had made as he fell. As if led by an invisible hand, she walked over to the bookcase and took the Bible off the shelf. She folded her hands on the cover and felt the tears fall on her fingers.

"Lord God," she prayed, "you know I've read this book almost every day since I learned to read. I've heard of people opening the Bible in time of need and getting a direct word from you. I confess I've always thought that was sort of superstitious nonsense. I'm really sorry. They must have felt like I do right now. I need to hear from you, God. Please help me."

Mary opened the Bible.

Psalm 40

I waited patiently for the Lord; he inclined to me and heard my cry. He drew me up from the desolate pit, out of the miry bog, and set my feet upon a rock, making my steps secure. He put a new song in my mouth, a song of praise to our God. Many will see and fear, and put their trust in the Lord.

Mary began to feel a surge of excitement. Some of the phrases seemed to shoot out at her as if underlined.

Blessed is the man who makes the Lord his trust....

She read over and over the words that said:

Sacrifice and offering thou dost not desire; but thou hast given me an open ear. Burnt offering and sin offering thou hast not required. Then I said, "Lo, I come; in the roll of the book it is written of me; I delight to do thy will, O my God; thy law is within my heart."

The ice began to melt just a little.

Do not thou, O Lord, withhold thy mercy from me, let thy steadfast love and thy faithfulness ever preserve me!

The Psalm finished with words that were already in Mary's heart:

As for me, I am poor and needy; but the Lord takes thought for me. Thou art my help and my deliverer; do not tarry, O my God!

She looked out the window. New snow sparkled on the fields. The moon seemed to be lighting the scene just for her. She thought of the words she had just read. "Sacrifice and offering thou dost not desire; but thou hast given me an open ear."

The river drew a question mark in the snow as it rounded the bend and disappeared behind the hill. It seemed a reflection of her own questions. What is an open ear? Is it one tuned in to God, to hear what he has to tell us about our lives? How could a brain tumor relate to that? Was there something God wanted to say to her in the Psalm she had just read, if she could be perceptive enough to hear? Her eyes searched the moonlit fields as if to help her spirit move out beyond them.

Her memory roamed back to the time when she was twenty, in nursing school, and loving it in spite of the hard work. She awoke one morning with a sore throat. Twenty-four hours later she was lying in the cell-like room in the Isolation Hospital, her diaphragm half paralyzed, her breathing muscles completely useless. The diagnosis on the chart at the nurses' station read: "Bulbar-spinal poliomyelitis. Condition, critical."

A dog barked far off in the distance. She thought of her father's words as he was driving her home from the hospital five months later. "The doctor said only five percent of the patients with bulbar polio live. He said you had too much guts to die. Then they told us there was no chance that you could recover the use of all of your muscles. He didn't think you'd be able to walk for two years."

Mary recalled the sense of ineffable peace that had filled her body, mind, and spirit every afternoon in the hospital when she heard a church bell peal somewhere. She had never told anybody. The words of the Twenty-third Psalm had seemed to ring out in her, even though she didn't have breath to say them.

> The Lord is my shepherd, I shall not want;
> he makes me lie down in green pastures. He leads me beside still waters; he restores my soul.
> He leads me in paths of righteousness for his name's sake.
> Even though I walk through the valley of the shadow of death, I fear no evil; for thou art with me; thy rod and thy staff, they comfort me.
> Thou preparest a table before me in the presence of my enemies;
> thou anointest my head with oil, my cup overflows.
> Surely goodness and mercy shall follow me all the days of my life;
> and I shall dwell in the house of the Lord for ever.

"I couldn't lift my arms or legs or move my body or even clear my throat, but I never doubted that I would be all right, God. Where is that faith now? Where did it go?" Her hand rubbed the windowsill as she prayed, as though touching the firm wood could bring faith back to her.

She thought of the first day of their honeymoon, five

years later. They were on a quick trip to California, but her new husband had driven down a marked trail in the Ozark mountains, willing to spend a few extra hours to find a cozy cabin in the woods. Early the next morning he had said, "You start out driving this morning. We'll see how it works out best."

She recalled the next voice she'd heard, a week later. "I don't know how you can be alive, young lady. It's a miracle. You have two skull fractures. Your brain was so swollen when we X-rayed your head that there was a quarter-inch separation of the fragments. You have a lower occipital fracture and a left frontal fracture. Those are two extremely vital areas of the brain. How the hemorrhaging didn't kill you, I'll never know."

"A miracle." The words seemed to ring out now in the empty room. "God, forgive me. I never even realized what a miracle that was until this very moment. I never even wrote to thank that minister who came every day and prayed for me to recover. I think I still have his card in my recipe file." She got up. It was there. "I wonder if you're still alive, Reverend Russell Jay of the First Congregational Church in Lebanon, Missouri. Where are you right now? I wish I could tell you thank you."

Her thoughts went back to a time several months after the accident. They had settled into their apartment in Milwaukee. She had started to feel numbness in her legs and tingling in her arms.

"My dear girl," the orthopedic man had said, "you have cracked ribs, fractured cervical and sacral vertebrae. Didn't they even X-ray you down there in Missouri? We're going to have to put a Thomas collar on you to prevent more deterioration of the intervertebral discs."

"Please, God, don't make me wear one of those awful collars," she had prayed as the yellow and black Ford drove back through busy traffic. "I can't waste the time, God. I want to have a baby." Tears rolled down her cheeks. "I told that doctor to give me two weeks. But I'm never going back, God. Please heal me. You let me throw away that dumb brace those doctors said I'd have to wear all my life after I had polio. I remember the day I got so sick of strapping myself in that thing that I threw it in the corner. You let me keep it off. Please, God, we both want to have a baby."

Her mind traveled from past to present. "You let us have the baby, God. And now they tell us he was born with a brain tumor. Why, God?"

Mary heard a soft step. She turned to see Scott, his hand on the banister, walking slowly down the stairs. He walked across the room to his mother, stood looking at her, and finally said in a voice almost too soft to hear, "Mom, I'm scared."

Mary stood up. She put her arms around her son and tucked his head under her chin, hugging him tight. She swallowed hard, willing the tears to stay back. "I'm scared too, Scott."

She put her arm around his shoulders as they walked together into the kitchen and sat down at the round table. "Scott, there's something in here that's always helped me when I had problems. Maybe it will help you right now."

Mary picked up the Bible as she spoke, opening it to the Twenty-third Psalm. Her voice took on authority as she read the familiar phrases.

Scott's eyes were soft and thoughtful as his mother looked up from the Bible. "You know, Mother, what this reminds me of? It's like the night I was inducted into the Order of the Arrow in the Boy Scouts. I had to go out in the woods alone, to sleep. It was raining, and I was afraid." Scott's back straightened. "Mother, do you know what this is going to be? It's going to be an emotionally maturing experience for me."

CHAPTER TWO

"BE STILL"

Like busy sparrows, the waitresses were cleaning up the hospital coffee shop in the afternoon on December 24. Mary sat at the counter, a half-empty cup of coffee in front of her as she watched the snow driving against the windows.

The blonde woman sitting across the U-shaped counter caught her eye. "Fine way to spend Christmas Eve, isn't it?" Mary nodded. The woman went on, "I've been in here every day for two months. My husband had a brain tumor removed six weeks ago."

"He did? Why, my son has a brain tumor. Who's your doctor?"

"Dr. Levin. Who's yours?"

"Dr. Levin. How do you like him?"

The woman picked up her cup and moved over next to Mary. "There's nobody like him! We've been going from doctor to doctor for five years to find out why my husband was having convulsions. They all said it was epilepsy. They gave him medicine to control the convulsions, but they just kept getting worse. They all said there was no evidence of brain tumor. Dr. Levin found it right away." She put her cup down hard.

She stopped talking, sat silently looking into the face so close to her own. Her penetrating blue eyes made Mary uncomfortable. "I know how you feel. You're scared, aren't you? Real scared." Her neck craned, like that of an inquisitive goose. Mary turned away quickly to hide the rush of tears the statement evoked. Her inquisitor refused to be put off. "Have you tried praying?"

Mary could only nod her head. She felt in the pockets of her sweater for her handkerchief.

"But have you really prayed?" The mouth twisted, as she relentlessly repeated the phrase. "Have you really prayed? Have you been in the chapel? Come on. You and I are going in there to pray, right now."

She clamped her lips tightly together as she jabbed out her cigarette in the ashtray. As Mary scrubbed at her eyes, the woman picked up their checks and went over to the cash register.

They sat in the softly lit chapel. Mary felt a warm hand cover her cold one. She made no attempt to wipe away the tears that ran down her cheeks and was only dimly aware when the woman left the room.

She kept her eyes on the picture of Christ kneeling in the garden, inlaid high on the wall in stained glass. As she looked at it, the light that shone above the altar seemed to grow brighter. She opened her eyes wide as the glow seemed to penetrate her and light up the inside of her head with a clear, pure intensity. She sat very still.

As she walked back to the elevator, she looked around the hospital lobby, trying to discern the difference she felt. Was it in the hospital atmosphere itself, or was it in her? Scott opened his eyes as she came into his room.

"Where were you, Mom? You've been gone a long time."

"Have I, Scott? I didn't realize it. I was down in the chapel."

"What were you doing in the chapel?"

"I was praying." She sat down by the bed. "You know, Scott, I found out this afternoon that I really don't know much about prayer. I've been going in that chapel every day and it wasn't doing me a bit of good. I found out why today. I've always talked to God. I didn't know he could talk to me."

"Did he talk to you today?"

"Yes, I think he did."

"What did he say?" The eyelids that had seemed so heavy opened a little wider. The eyes looked more alive.

"I think he said, 'Be still and know that I am God. Be still.' That means just what it says. Rest. Relax. Unclench your teeth. Turn off your mind. Quit asking questions."

"And did you?"

"I did. It really worked. I felt myself relax all over. My body went limp. My toes even wiggled."

"Gee, that's really neat, Mom. I'm going to do that when I have to go in to have my operation. I've been kind of worrying about that."

Mary got up from the chair by Scott's bed and walked to the window. Blowing snow obscured the street lights far below. Large white drifts were forming on the roof beneath the window.

The nurse came in and handed Scott a little plastic cup. "Here, Scott, take these pills. It's pretty bad out there, Mrs. Soergel. At least half the nurses called in to say they can't get in. They're canceling Christmas Eve services all over town."

"When do you think Dad will be here, Mother?"

"I don't know. He should be in by now. I suppose the snow is slowing down the trains too."

Mary looked up to see Scott's eyelids drooping.

"Go to sleep if you feel like it, Scott. I'll wake you when your dad gets here."

"OK, Mom. Do me a favor first, will you? Please read me the Twenty-third Psalm again."

Reading through the Psalm, Mary could only whisper the words, "Even though I walk through the valley of the shadow of death, I fear no evil." She looked at Scott, hoping he hadn't caught her feelings. She need not have worried. Scott's eyes were closed. His chest moved up and down in a slow and even rhythm.

Mary heard voices singing. She stood up and walked to

the door. The nurse had told her the cast of "Brigadoon" was coming to the hospital, but she had thought surely the snow would keep them away. She had been mistaken. As they walked toward her down the hall, their fur coats, high boots, and scarves flung dramatically around their necks lent an air of reality to the music they sang. Mary stepped back into the shadows as the tall soprano, joined by the heavier voice of the man walking beside her, started the title song just as they reached Scott's door. They both turned their heads, looked in at the face of the boy whose eyelids did not even flicker in response to the beauty of their song.

The symbolism of the story stabbed into Mary as they walked away. They left behind them the echoes of the lovely town that rose for just one day, then sank back into oblivion.

Tears blurred the white figures at the nurses' station as Mary ran down the hall. She pushed open the door marked "Ladies." She pulled a paper towel from the silver container on the wall. It felt cold to her hand as she brushed against it. She put the towel over her eyes, leaned her head against the wall, and gave way to her feelings. Her shoulders shuddered as she sobbed, forgetting completely the end of the Twenty-third Psalm: "Surely goodness and mercy shall follow me all the days of my life; and I will dwell in the house of the Lord for ever."

CHAPTER THREE

IS HUNTINGTON'S DISEASE HEREDITARY?

The hospital room was quiet as Mary entered and hung her coat in the closet. Scott's eyes remained closed. He seemed unaware of his mother's presence. Mary sat down in the big chair in the corner of the room. She reached in her knitting bag for the mail she had taken from the mailbox on the way to the hospital. Christmas cards. The one from her sister-in-law had a folded piece of paper with a note in Gayle Soergel's slanting, backhand writing.

Dear Mary,
  I wish you were closer. I need to talk to someone. Ed has been having some very strange symptoms for quite a long time. His coordination has been slipping. He falls and drops things. His mind doesn't seem quite as sharp as it was. He reads less. He seems worried, strangely cross. He didn't want to see the doctor, but I insisted he see a neurologist. He went yesterday. The doctor said he couldn't find a thing wrong with him.
  Mary, did anyone ever say anything to you about Huntington's chorea being hereditary? We know their dad died of it. Did any of the rest of the family? How many were there? I seem to remember hearing there were seven of them. What happened to them all? They were all dead by the time we were married. Did you ever know any of them? If I ask Ed he says

31

"I don't know" or "I don't remember." Does Norm ever talk about any of his father's family? Does he ever talk about his father?

Mary, I'm really worried about Ed. He's not the beautiful man I married. I know there is something the matter with him. I don't believe that doctor.

"Mrs. Soergel." Startled, Mary looked up at the nurse that stood beside Scott's bed. "You asked me about Dr. Levin. He just came on the floor. He should be in to see Scott before he leaves."

Mary jammed the letter down inside her purse. The urgency of her own need to talk to the doctor about Scott erased from her mind the questions the letter had raised. She hit the doctor with her questions as soon as he walked in the door.

He put his hand up in front of his face as if to ward off the force of the words. "Mrs. Soergel, Mrs. Soergel, one at a time." He took hold of her arm, gave her a reassuring pat. "Nothing you ate, dreamed, smoked, or thought caused that brain tumor in your son."

"My husband's father died of some strange disease the family doesn't like to talk about, called Huntington's chorea. Could that have any connection?"

Mary watched the doctor's face closely for any reaction. She tried to read his expression.

He looked noncommitally at her. "No. We don't know what causes these tumors. I wish we did."

"If we had caught it sooner, would he have had a better chance?"

"Of course." The doctor's eyes looked thoughtful. "But these tumors are very difficult ones to diagnose. Didn't you wonder why Scott didn't grow? You said he bought size five shoes the last two years. That's a rather small size for a fourteen-year-old boy. Didn't you think that strange?"

"No." Mary felt put on the defensive. "My father was so

small that he graduated from high school in his first pair of long pants. I grew tall after I was sixteen. Norm also grew later than average. We thought it just a part of the family pattern. We're really thankful, though, that the tumor isn't malignant."

The doctor looked at her silently for a moment. "No, it isn't malignant in the sense that it could ever turn into another kind of tumor or spread to other organs. It is malignant, however, to the degree that if it isn't encapsulated, it will continue to grow. Only one out of a hundred is encapsulated."

"What difference does that make?"

"It means that we might not be able to get it all out. A very vital area of the brain is involved. The pituitary gland is the master gland of the body. It's already affected. Proof is Scott's size, his abnormally undeveloped bone structure. What other damage has been done we have no way of knowing until we do the final tests."

"When will you be doing those?"

"We do the arteriogram tomorrow. This is a surgical procedure. Please stop at the nurses' station to sign the consent form before you leave tonight."

"What is an arteriogram?"

"It charts the course of the blood supply in the brain. We inject dye into the carotid artery in his neck. By looking at the blood supply we can discover the extent of the tumor's progression."

"When will you operate?"

"Several days after the arteriogram. Scott's neck will be quite painful and swollen. We'll wait until the swelling subsides."

"Is that the last test you'll do before surgery?"

"We do a pneumoencephalogram the day of surgery; *pneumo* means the injection of air. This procedure will allow us to see the shape of the tumor. We'll photograph Scott's head after the air is injected."

After the doctor left the room, the questions in Gayle's

letter nagged at Mary, like a ball of yarn that had been pulled out and tangled with the threads of her fear for Scott. She was anxious to put them back where they belonged in the bottom of her knitting bag.

"Norm," she began when he picked her up at the hospital later. "We had a letter from Gayle in our Christmas card."

"Oh? What did she say?"

"She said she was worried about Ed. She asked me all kinds of questions." She waited.

"What kind of questions?" His voice had taken on a guarded tone.

"About your father, about..."

"Just a minute." His right hand left the steering wheel, cutting the air with a quick jabbing wave. He reached over and switched on the transistor radio balanced on the dashboard of the car. "I want to hear what the weather is going to do."

Mary's eyes narrowed. She felt his hand cutting her off, almost physically. She took a deep breath and as she released it, she canceled the words she had been rehearsing in her mind to tell her husband, the words the doctor had said about Scott. She looked out the car window as the voice of the newscaster changed to music and Norm remained silent. She had never felt more alone.

CHAPTER FOUR

NOT OURS TO KEEP

Scott grinned at his parents as they walked into his hospital room the day of surgery. "Look at my neck. The swelling is all gone. No more elephant neck."

Their roles seemed reversed. He took the place of the comforting, supporting parent; they the children that needed him to be stable and calm. He steered the conversation, skillfully avoiding emotional overtones until the nurse walked into the room, syringe in hand.

The two hours seemed like twenty as they waited for the doctor to tell them what he had found. When he did come for them, it was a different Dr. Levin. His usual grin was replaced by a grim and almost forbidding expression. He put the large negatives he was carrying into the viewer against the wall, turned on the light behind them, picked up the pointer, and gestured at the film. It looked like heavy storm clouds, indistinctly blended with lighter clouded areas superimposed over the outlines of a skull.

"Here is the tumor." He touched the film with the pointer. "Here, and here, and here."

Mary glanced with bewilderment at her husband. Did he see what the doctor was trying to show them?

"Look." The pointer touched the top of the skull, which had an obvious crack. "You can see the size of it by the way it's made the segments of the skull separate. If Scott were adult, his headaches would have been excruciating. His bone structure has been so severely retarded that the skull fragments separated like those of a baby."

He took down the films and put them in a large Manila envelope. "Now I'm going to go in and try to get that thing out of there."

Mary held out to him the index card she was carrying. Her father had brought it over to their house the night before and had handed it to her without a word. The surgeon read it to himself.

> Gracious Lord and heavenly father, we commend to your watch and care this day our beloved grandson, Scott. We thank you for him, and for what he has meant to us and to all those who love him. We pray that your blessing may continue to fall on him, that he may be fully conscious of your love and care for him. So may it be with us all. Our faith and our trust are in you, that you may restore him soon to full health and strength. May your will be done. This we pray in the name of Jesus Christ our Lord.

Dr. Levin handed the card back to Mary. His face was guarded, his eyes unreadable. "From now on, it's in God's hands," he said.

Dr. Levin's usual brisk walk was slow, his shoulders drooped as he walked into the room and sat on the bed. "It was a bad one. How long were we in there? About five hours, I guess. It was full of green, greasy fluid. We aspirated out as much as we could, cut away as much of the capsule as we could see."

Mary didn't have to ask the question that was in her mind. He had already answered it. The tumor was not encapsulated.

Dr. Levin pulled off the green skull cap he wore. "So far he's doing very well. The next forty-eight hours will be the critical ones. There may have been damage to the hypothalamus. This tiny gland lies at the base of the pituitary stalk. It's the seat of emotional control—controls body temp and water metabolism—so it's a pretty important little fellow. Scott's temperature could become very erratic. So far it hasn't. Damage to the hypothalamus can also cause a kind of diabetes. There are two kinds of diabetes, diabetes mellitus, the more common 'sugar diabetes'..." He looked over at Mary. He knew her nursing background. "Do you remember the other kind?"

Words came to her from out of the past. "Diabetes insipidus?"

"That's right." He nodded approvingly, looked at Norm. "You've a smart wife. We'll have to watch the urine output closely. Scott could start urinating copiously, causing dehydration, electrolyte imbalance." He looked at both parents, shaking his head. "I sure wish we knew what causes these awful tumors in these little guys." He jumped down off the bed. "Would you like to see him? He's in the recovery room. I'm going up there right now. You can go with me if you'd like."

Mary stood up eagerly. "Sure."

The doctor looked inquiringly at Norm, who shook his head. "No thanks. I'll wait until he's back down here."

The doctor and Mary were the only people in the elevator marked "Use for Surgical Patients Only."

Dr. Levin looked at her, his eyes serious. "This reminds me of a story, Mrs. Soergel. It's a story about a ruler who was going away on a long trip. He had a very precious pearl. He looked for someone to take care of his pearl for him while he was gone. He left it with two of his most trusted subjects, whom he loved very much and knew he could depend on. He came back eighteen years later, but when he went to reclaim his pearl, they didn't want to give it up. They had taken such good care of it, they thought it was their own. So the ruler said to them, 'I didn't say it was yours to keep, did I?' " He faced Mary, took both of her arms in his hands, and held them firmly. "Do you know what I mean?"

Mary looked at the granite-grey eyes questioning hers. "Yes, Dr. Levin, I know what you mean."

She steeled herself to face the worst as they entered the recovery room. Green-gowned figures walked quickly between the beds. Scott's head was wrapped with a large, white turbanlike bandage. Needles in both forearms were attached to tubes dangling from hanging bottles. Blood dripped slowly from one; the other contained a yellowish liquid. A tube snaked from beneath the bed covers to a bottle on the floor. Scott opened his eyes as his mother walked up to his bed.

"Hi, Mom. How are you?" he said in a completely normal tone of voice.

Almost too shocked to talk, Mary gasped, "I'm fine, Scott. How are you?"

"Oh, my head hurts a little. Otherwise I feel great." His smile looked a little lopsided. His face was starting to swell.

The doctor looked inquiringly at the nurse who was taking a blood pressure cuff from his arm.

She smiled. "Blood pressure normal. Pulse and respiration normal. Temperature normal. Urine output normal." She gave Scott's arm a pat. "You're a very normal young man, aren't you, Scott?"

Ten days later Mary sang as the shower spray pelted her back. Getting ready for bed, she remembered the doctor saying good-bye to Scott that morning. "Scott, you bounced back from brain surgery as if it were no more than an appendectomy."

She rummaged in her disorganized top drawer for pencil and paper, sat on her bed, and wrote out a poem as it came to her.

> He lives!
> For all the world to see
> The essence of Christianity.
> God's saving grace, his power, his light
> Have led our steps past death's dark night,

And turned our quivering mass of fear
To faith that Jesus Christ is here.
Our thanks to him who lets us be
A vessel on life's stormy sea,
Whose faith and hope and love prevail,
Though winds of death tear at our sail,
To chart the course for those less strong,
Who have not known our Christ as long.
Our compass is a cross of wood
Which on the hill of Calvary stood.
Our needle is a bloody thorn
From out his brow so cruelly torn.
Our anchor is a stone of grey
From death's dark tomb once rolled away.
Lord, if we falter, lift us up,
Hold to our lips thy healing cup,
Thy chalice full of love so pure,
That once again, replete, secure,
We'll lift our hearts in faith, set free,
To witness, Christ our Lord, to thee.

CHAPTER FIVE

FALTERING

For a few months, Mary didn't think much. She didn't have time. She was too tired. It was a scramble getting her work done in time to take Scott the forty miles into Milwaukee every day for the cobalt treatment. She left Ebbie guarding the sleeping Becca in the car as she and Scott went into the hospital for what seemed like a ridiculously short treatment. Mary breathed a silent prayer each time the doctor aimed the deadly machine at the square he had crayoned on Scott's temple. What if it should miss the mark? She had closed her mind to the implications in the warnings the doctor had given her before he began the treatments. It had all seemed a jumble of doomful words such as "scar tissue," "epilepsy," "blindness," "the lesser of two evils." She had felt like screaming at him, "Shut up."

After the seven weeks of cobalt were finished, Scott went back to school. As the other kids rode the bus, he insisted that he was going to ride his bike. He was determined to get strong as soon as possible. He gave hardly any signs that he had been ill, except for the bald spots on his temples, heritage of the cobalt.

Mary wished, as the months went by, that she could forget as quickly as Scott. As she lay awake at night, she thought back to the simplicity of their life before they had found out about Scott's tumor, and wondered why Norman was spending so much more time away from home.

She thought of how differently she felt about all the children younger than Scott. She had changed drastically her attitudes about their achievements. She could care less. She didn't care what grades they got, if they practiced their musical instruments, if they went to Boy Scouts and Girl Scouts. She was simply thankful that they were healthy. She stood by the kitchen window almost every day as they got off the school bus, glorying in their obvious abundance of health, the color in their faces, their strong muscles as they ran through the front yard.

Her feelings about her own activities had changed as drastically. The interests she had formerly found so fascinating seemed dull and boring. The City Plan Commission she had been flattered to join at the invitation of the mayor seemed a jumble of senseless conversation about nothing. The Girl Scout leader's job she had found a challenge seemed senseless, as if the things that were offered the girls were not really very important. She stopped attending the meetings of the League of Women Voters. She still went to PTA, but it held no interest for her; she went because she thought it her parental duty.

She spent more time alone. She avoided the morning and afternoon coffee with her neighbors whenever she could. When she felt she could not bow out gracefully, their talk bored her.

She felt a strange, constantly smoldering anger. She hated to grocery shop. Every store seemed filled with people as impersonal as the cans on the shelves. She felt like pushing her grocery cart into every other cart she met.

She played the piano a lot. She dug out the books that were too difficult for her to play. She found a mystifying satisfaction in the chords of the masters, as she pounded them out on the keys.

She read copiously. The Bible that had been her daily companion for a short period each day became a fascinating friend. She ate up the pages with her eyes. It seemed to share her feelings more intimately than any human, except for the author John Gunther. One night after she had finished his book *Death Be Not Proud*, she sat down to write to him. Tears dripped on the sheets of unmatched paper she pulled from the cupboard in the kitchen as she told him of the similarity in their sons. She had been unable to put down the book after she started the story of John Gunther Jr.'s valiant struggle with death, lost to the creeping malignancy that ate up his brain.

The darkness of that night was far from her mind one sunny day when she walked out to the mailbox to find a large white envelope with the words "John Gunther, 1 East Avenue, New York 21, New York" printed in the upper left hand corner. The word AIRMAIL was printed in bright blue ink in large capital letters, underlined twice. Unbelieving, she put her finger under the flap and pulled out the sheet of paper. She read as she walked back towards the house.

> Dear Mrs. Soergel:
>
> I am so sorry to be this late answering your letter of September 25th. I have just this week finished a very long book, and my mail has had to accumulate until it is quite an unmanageable pile.
>
> I was deeply moved and touched by what you said in your letter. I know what you and your husband are going through, and believe me you have my heartfelt sympathy for it all. If *Death Be Not Proud* has given you any kind of comfort or courage, I am grateful. It was really Johnny's book, not mine.
>
> Yours most sincerely,
> John Gunther

Mary felt strangely comforted. She didn't show the letter to Norman when he came home from work. She was afraid he would be angry with her.

Mary lay in bed thinking about *Death Be Not Proud*. She thought of all the different attempts the Gunthers had made to save the life of their son, going from doctor to doctor. The book had brought back to her the question that had so often crossed her mind since Dr. Levin had

told her the story in the elevator—"should we consult another doctor?" She had never discussed the question with
Norman. Reinforced by the sincerity of the letter she had
received, she determined to try. She jumped out of bed,
wrapping her robe around her. She walked down the
stairs, into the kitchen, where her husband sat, beer glass
in hand. She walked up to stand beside him.

"Norm, I want to talk to you."

Norman's eyebrows met in a sharp wedge, the lines in
his forehead cut deep.

"What about?"

Mary took a deep breath. She looked at her husband's
frowning face. She blurted out the words she had been
wanting to say for a long time.

"Do you think we should take Scott to another doctor
while there's still time?"

He raised the magazine like a shield in front of his
chest. His eyes squinted at her over the top of it.

"What do you mean, 'While there's still time'?"

"You remember the story Dr. Levin told me in the
elevator, about the ruler who left his pearl..."

The knife blade of his voice cut into her sentence.

"Damn Dr. Levin. I never did like him."

Norman grabbed for a can of beer, picking up the
opener with his left hand. She felt, as well as heard, the
defiant hiss as he opened the can.

"Get another doctor if you want. They're all a bunch of
fakes anyway."

Mary ran from the room.

Her body felt stiff when she woke from a dream, hours
later. She listened to the whine of the wind as it whistled
around the corner of the house, in duet with the deep
snoring breaths of her husband. She felt cold as the dream
replayed itself in her mind, like a movie reel that repeated
itself on a screen she could not escape. She saw herself in
the car as it sped down the steep hill, leading to a tunnel at
its foot. She saw the lineup of cars waiting to get through

the tunnel. She felt her foot as it touched the brake. Her stomach dropped in reaction to the fear she felt when she woke up just as she realized the brakes had failed and she was hurtling toward certain destruction.

Her mind lunged toward God as her body lay stiff with cold. Slowly she felt the spiritual vacuum sweeper pick her off the bed. The snoring faded. The whine of the wind diminished to a shrill whistle, then faded away. Her body relaxed to a limp warmth. She lay very still for a long time.

She slipped out of bed and reached for her robe. Without turning on the light, she groped in the drawer for her notebook and pencil. Out in the hall, she turned on the light and sat down on the floor, leaning back against the wall. She began to write, the notebook on her knees.

> "Ask what you will, I'll do for thee,
> Whatever you would ask of me.
> Just let me live, great God above,
> Within the shadow of thy love."
> These words I prayed, on bended knee,
> When first I gave my life to thee.
> When first I took the bread and wine,
> I swore my life was wholly thine.
> Now that I see my destiny,
> The shadow of Gethsemane,
> My crown of thorns is pressing tight,
> The cross I bear no longer light.
> Sweet Jesus, place thy hand in mine.
> When the sun's rays no longer shine,
> Light up my days of dark despair,
> With light of love, proof that you care,
> 'Til once again my faith is strong,
> And my heart sings the victory song,
> Whose words ring out so loud and clear,
> To comfort those who will but hear,
> "A few short years I ask from thee,
> But my gift is Eternity."

CHAPTER SIX

WHERE ARE YOUR CHILDREN?

"Mary, have you seen this?" The neighbor who had come in for a quick cup of coffee held out a *Time* magazine.

"Yes, I was looking at it at Betty Schumann's last night. You mean the article about the proton beam?"

"Yes. That's just what I do mean. Listen, Mary." She read, "It may be as vastly complex as the proton gun currently being used by Harvard neurosurgeons Raymond Kjellberg and William Sweet. Using a 700-ton magnet, Harvard's cyclotron fires a proton beam with the force of 160 million electron volts. After leaving the cyclotron, the protons travel an absolutely precise and predictable distance before they release their power. Careful positioning of the patient allows the patient little damage as the beam pierces the skin before releasing all its energy and destroying a specific target deep inside the body, such as the pituitary gland, perhaps, or a brain tumor."

Rae's face was serious. "Mary, why don't you take Scott to see those doctors? I don't believe that he's as healthy as you keep saying he is. I know they don't give thirty-five doses of cobalt to benign tumors."

Mary ignored the implication. "But, Rae, you can't just write to any old doctor you read about in a magazine and say, 'Please see my son.' Not when another neurosurgeon has already operated. I think doctors are quite careful not to infringe on each other's practice."

"Well then, ask Dr. Levin to refer you."

"I'll admit I thought of that when I read the article. I even asked Norm what he thought about it."

"What did he say?"

"He said, 'Do what you think best.' "

"Then what are you waiting for?"

"I guess I hate to do it because Scott is doing so well. If we went to another doctor, what would we tell Scott? He assumes that everything is all right. We'd have to tell him that Dr. Levin said the tumor would recur. I hate to do that to him."

"Then don't tell him."

"He's too smart to fool. I asked Dr. Levin what we should say if Scott asked and he said, 'Don't ever lie to him.' Then we'd have to tell everybody else too. I'm afraid of what people would say to Scott. He's been so brave about it all. You know how people talk and how they always exaggerate. I don't want anyone getting him all shook."

Rae was persistent. "How long does the doctor say he'll live?"

"Eighteen."

"Eighteen! That's not very far off. You're right. Scott is smart. Don't you think he'll be able to figure it out himself when he starts to feel like he did before?"

"I know he's going to have to know sooner or later. I just want it to be later."

Rae picked up the magazine, rolling it in her hands. "But if this proton thing worked, it wouldn't have to be *ever*. Wouldn't it be better for him to know there was a possibility of recurrence but you were doing something to prevent it, rather than realizing it himself and thinking there was nothing that could be done for him?"

Convinced by that logic, Mary sat down after Rae left and wrote to Dr. Levin.

In the next few weeks she kept very busy. She started keeping a daily journal as a way to straighten out her thinking. She started looking at everybody around her with a more inquisitive eye. What was beneath their surface? If she poked a hole in their veneer, would she find emotions as deep as she was hiding behind her own smile?

As the holiday season approached, Mary began to experience feelings of relief. She had heard nothing from any doctors. Her shot in the dark had missed the mark, she thought. Then Dr. Levin sent her a letter he had received from the Massachusetts General Hospital, recommending that Scott be brought there for testing. That same day Mary received a letter from that hospital giving the expected costs for Scott's hospitalization and care. Mary's eyes widened as she realized the least expensive bed was listed as "Ward: $52."

She waited until all the children were sleeping before going into the kitchen where her husband was reading the paper, glass in hand.

Mary handed Norm the letters and sat down opposite him at the table.

He read through them in silence. "What about it?" His eyes were clouded as he looked at his wife.

"Do you think we should go?"

"What do you think?"

"I don't know."

His tone softened as he saw she was close to tears. "I don't know, Mare. You're the nurse. If you think you should go, go."

"But what about the money?"

"Don't you worry about the money. Let me take care of the money, will you please?"

"But I can't help but worry. We don't have any saved. What are we going to use for transportation?"

"Borrow some. Go down to the bank tomorrow and get as much as you think you'll need."

"But I have no idea how much that is. I'll need some to

live on while Scott's in the hospital. How much do you think?"

Norm reached over, turned up his transistor. "Just a minute, I want to see what the weather is going to do tomorrow."

Mary bit her lip.

"I don't know, Mare. Start with $600. I can always send you more. What are you going to do? Fly?"

"It's a lot cheaper by train, with our railroad pass. I called the travel bureau today. It would cost over $200 plane fare one way for both of us. We can both go by train for $47. We'd get one-way tickets, so if he isn't feeling strong afterwards, we could fly back. I imagine the proton beam would be more tiring than cobalt, and that really knocked him out."

"Have you said anything to Scott yet?" Norm scratched a match under the kitchen table and lit a cigarette.

"No. I wanted to talk to you about it first. How are we going to tell him?"

"Just tell him, I guess."

"When do you have to go back to work?"

"Tomorrow night sometime. Why?" He flicked his ashes into the empty beer can.

"Why don't we take him out to eat tomorrow and tell him then? That way the other kids won't be popping in."

The restaurant noise seemed to insulate Mary from her own feelings. Scott ate his steak enthusiastically, surprised and pleased at the unexpected treat of dinner out with his parents, alone.

Mary looked across the table at Norm as the waitress put some apple pie down in front of Scott.

He picked up the signal. "Scott, your mother has been in touch with Dr. Levin. They think you should go to Boston to another hospital to see another doctor."

Scott put his fork down. He looked at his mother, his expression puzzled. "Why? I feel fine."

"Dr. Levin said when he operated on you that there was a chance that the tumor might recur some day. That's why you had the cobalt. There's a doctor in Boston who has developed something more powerful than cobalt. It's called a proton beam. We thought it might be a good idea for this doctor—his name is Dr. Sweet—to examine you. Just to be on the safe side."

"Well, OK. That sounds smart. Are you going too, Mother?"

"Of course. We take the train out of here Christmas Day."

They changed trains in Chicago. Scott seemed to enjoy watching the winter scenery rush past, but it gave Mary a feeling of unreality. As the train clacked through the night, Mary could not sleep. She pictured the scene at the depot where the family had come down to see them off. She remembered Norm's apparent anger as he grabbed Becca's arm when the train pulled in. She recalled her daughter's sharp cry of pain. Her husband had not kissed her good-bye; instead they had glared at each other as she stepped onto the metal stairs leading into the train. She blamed him for the way her daughter clung to her neck, crying as her father pulled her away.

Mary's mind tried to walk back through the maze of the present to the clear path of the past. She skipped from the twisting tunnel with no light where she had to grope her way, back to the time when the light was clear and bright.

She pictured the scene with a sharply focusing camera. She saw herself lying on the sunporch of the house in Minnesota where they had lived when Gretchen was born. She felt the warm little body beside her. She heard her husband in the kitchen where he was preparing dinner, saw him walk into the dining room, heard him talk to the two little boys who had been helping him. He barked out the commands, his voice repressing a smile.

"Report." She saw the two straight backs march into the

dining room with a place mat apiece. She smiled in reflection as she saw them set up the table at their father's direction. She saw them the next day as her mind's camera snapped the shutter. The same two little forms followed their father around the yard as he mowed the lawn, matching every curve in the grass as it blew back on their legs.

As the train whistled around a curve Mary's feelings matched the notes. What had happened to the father who wanted his children with him wherever he went? Where did the man go who threw his sons into the air with joyful abandon? Why had Norm changed? She fell into fitful sleep.

The train was several hours late getting into Boston, past the time when they were supposed to call the hospital. But when the cab delivered them in front of the tall brick building and they passed through those large glass doors, they had no trouble at all registering Scott. He was assigned to one of the older buildings in the complex tied together by long balloon-like tunnels.

"The nurse said there wouldn't be any doctors around until after supper, Mom. Let's explore some."

"Hi, Scott." The girl looked up from the table where she sat working on a puzzle, a small boy on her lap. She wore a blue uniform. "My name's Jane. I'm the Play Lady."

"How did you know my name's Scott? What do Play Ladies do?"

"I just guessed, actually. I was expecting a new patient named Scott. Play Ladies do just that. They play."

"Do you play Scrabble?"

"We have a Scrabble board we share with the fifth floor. It's up there right now. I'll get it when I'm done here, and we can have a game."

Mary glanced at her watch. "I hate to do it, Scott, but I think I'd better go. Happy's dad said he couldn't come get me because he can't go out in this kind of weather with his emphysema. He told me how to get to his apartment in

Cambridge, but you know I've never even seen a subway."

"Sure, Mom. I'll be fine. I'll have fun beating Jane in a game of Scrabble. Come on, I'll walk you to the elevator."

Mary stood by tracks that gleamed in the light of the setting sun, trying to decipher the directions she had scribbled on the envelope she held. "Let's see, which way is north? I guess I'll just get on the first train that comes by and ask if it's headed north."

"No, lady," said the man whose elbow jammed into her ribs, "you're going the wrong way. Get off at the next stop. Go down the stairs, through the tunnel, wait at the lower level, and take the train marked 'Harvard Square.' "

The subway screeching around the curves in the dark tunnel matched the feeling in Mary's head. She watched the signs on the walls at each stop. Finally she saw the one her host had mentioned. She asked the motorman to be sure.

"Yes, lady, here's where you catch the bus to Cambridge."

She walked up the stairs. Her eyes blinked though the sun had set; the twilight haze seemed bright in contrast to the subway tunnel.

Mary breathed a sigh of relief when she saw the number on the tall brick apartment building as she walked down Massachusetts Avenue after getting off the bus.

The inflection in the voice of the tall man who stepped from the elevator welcomed her as he said, "You must be Mary. I'm so glad to have you here. Let me take your bag."

Mary looked longingly at the bed as her friend's father led her to the room that would be hers. She resisted the temptation to drop down on it. She changed into the new tan wool slacks she had bought before leaving home.

As she rode the increasingly familiar bus and subway routes, Mary became grateful for Harry's friendship that started that evening in his apartment. She could realize, from the note of welcome in his voice that greeted her each evening when she stepped through the door, how lonely he was. She enjoyed listening to him tell her of his life, from a lonely little boy, through Harvard into France and the First World War up to the present. She sipped Coke and ate crackers and olives, forgetting momentarily the bedroom at the hospital beside the river on Charles Street.

The young doctor's questions about the family medical history pestered Mary's mind as the subway screeched around the curves heading for Harvard Square.

"Your husband's father died of Huntington's disease?"

"Yes."

"Is your husband having periodic check-ups?"

"No."

"What did the other members of Mr. Soergel's father's family die from?"

"I don't know."

"How many of them were there in the family?"

"Seven, I think."

"And you don't know how any of them died?"

Mary tried to piece together the fragments she knew about Norm's father. They made an erratic picture of an emotionally unstable man who had, according to Norm's grandmother, been difficult to live with. She wished she had asked her mother-in-law more about her husband. Norm wouldn't, or couldn't, talk about his father. She had a shadowy memory of allusions to drunks and institutions. She shook her head, as if to shake off an irritating gnat. She reached in her purse for the letter that had come from Josh the day before. She forgot the doctor's questions as she pictured her son sitting at the kitchen table as he wrote.

Dear Mom,

I am going to write to Scott too. We all pray that he is going to be fine, and we know he is going to be. Everybody, I know, has a purpose in life for them to fulfill. Scott has a purpose in life. He has shown me and lots of people courage and braveness and he will go on and show other people this. I will try to write a poem about this and other things tonight. It is now eleven. I just got the feeling to write this letter.

Dad just got back from Marlene and Bill's. I enjoyed my peace and quiet while he was gone. Sometimes you just get the feeling you need to be alone. I think I get this feeling more and more now. I need to be alone or I think I would be in bad shape. The need to be alone is because you need to think things over and philosophize. Dad just went back to Bill's. Good. I need to be alone a while longer. You really realize when someone is gone how much you need them and miss them. However, we all realize that Scott needs you and that is where you should be, no matter what happens here.

I am sorry to burden you with my troubles, but somehow I don't think you will mind. After all, what are mothers for? On the radio they said, "It is now eleven o'clock, curfew time. Parents, do you know where your children are?" They should also have said, "It is now eleven o'clock. Children, do you know where your parents are?"

Love always,
Your son Josh

Several days later outside the X-ray unit in the hospital, Dr. Sweet's steel-grey eyes looked directly into Mary's as he talked. "Mrs. Soergel, the situation isn't quite as hopeless as we anticipated. It is not, however, one where we would use the proton beam. That would become a destructive process. But we have recently developed high-powered microscopes that make radical removal of pharyngiomas possible. I performed the first one on the sister of a friend who is a doctor. He begged me to try something more charitable than the procedures that had been done previously, such as trying to collapse the tumor into the sinus cavities. Our predictions are not as dolorous as they were when we did the first operations. We have done twelve, and there have been no fatalities. I'd like to operate on Scott."

Mary sat in shocked silence. Surgery had never entered her mind. The doctor looked at her speculatively. "I do have to caution you that the recovery period wouldn't be as simple as Scott's recuperation after the first operation. There's a greater danger of complications. We would try to save at least a part of the stalk of the pituitary. Scott, however, would never be able to sire a child." He paused. "Mrs. Soergel, if Scott were my boy, this is what I would do."

"I'd have to call my husband," Mary said finally. "When would you operate?"

"Nursing care is particularly vital after this kind of surgery. The nurses on Burnham four have asked to take care of Scott after surgery. They say he is a favorite, a very special boy. It would be better to wait until after the holiday week is over, so they'll be fully staffed. I think probably about Wednesday or Thursday of next week. You can let us know what you decide."

"Dr. Sweet," Mary said numbly, "Dr. Levin said Scott would live to be eighteen. Is that what your estimate would be if we decide not to operate?"

"Yes," he nodded. "I think that was a very honest estimate, give or take a year or two."

The people lining the corridors, lying on stretchers, sitting in wheelchairs, leaning against the wall began to blur into one indistinct smear as tears began their course down her face. She stopped at the phone booth across from the florist's. The saucy tulips in the pot on the cart outside the phone booth seemed to mock the tears as she dialed her home number.

It was Grandma Soergel answering the phone with her usual lilting "Hello."

"Hi, Gram. Is Norm home?"

"Oh, Mary. Norm, it's Mary. Yes, he's here. He just came in about ten minutes ago."

"Hi, Mare." Norm's warm voice coming across the line seemed very close.

"Norm, Dr. Sweet wants to operate on Scott." She spoke rapidly, as if she wanted to rid herself of the words. "He said this is a new operation they have developed, using high-powered microscopes."

"What about the proton beam?"

"He said they can't use that. He said it would be too destructive. He said if Scott were his son, this is what he would do."

"What do you think?"

"I never even thought of an operation when we came, did you?"

Norm's voice was emphatic. "No."

"I asked him how long it would be if they didn't operate."

"What did he say?"

"The same as Dr. Levin."

There was quite a long silence. Then Mary said softly, "I don't suppose we have any choice, do we?"

"No. I don't suppose we have."

Back at the apartment Mary slit open the envelope from Josh and pulled out the crumpled piece of paper that had been smoothed and folded.

> For he is my brother
> And I love him, like no other.
> Not out of pity, or sorrow,
> But I love him because he is my brother.
> I offer him a gift, a gift of prayer.
> And many times I've wondered, and asked God,
> Is it really fair?
> God sent him upon us for an example

Of steadfastness and courage.
Ah, is life only a mirage?
The power of God is so deep,
But life is not ours to keep,
Not out of pity, not out of sorrow,
But I love him because he is my brother.

Love,
Your son Joshua

CHAPTER SEVEN

DRIFTING APART

The day of surgery, Mary dropped to her knees at the altar in the quiet chapel. Her mind felt empty of words. Her eyes lifted to the octagonal window high in the wall, as if magnetically drawn by its blueness. Her ears were oblivious to any sound. She felt as if she were being extended, pulled fine and taut, then snapped into the depths of a world inside herself she had never encountered. She became unconscious of any sense of time or place.

"Fear not, for I have overcome the world." The words came all at once. She felt their force, as if they had been stamped on her brain in large, indelible capital letters.

She stood up and walked briskly from the chapel. She went up to Scott's room and put on her coat. She ran down the four flights of stairs and out into the street, where she joined the crowds on Charles Street. She felt released.

"God, give him courage, guide his hands, give him courage, guide his hands." She marched to the rhythm of the words as she walked across the Boston Public Gardens, past the pond where the swan boat glided in the summer. She almost ran through the paths emptied by the winter. "Help him to cut deep down, Lord. You be the scalpel." She saw nothing. She didn't feel the chill. Her awareness was totally immersed in the hospital surgery blocks away.

Six hours later, back in the hospital, she called her husband. "Norm, I just talked with Dr. Sweet. Scott's all right. He said it was his opinion that it was a satisfactory procedure." Then she added words she had anticipated. "He said they had scraped as close to the brain as they could with safety. The biopsy showed there are tumor cells remaining. He said he couldn't guarantee that the tumor wouldn't grow back."

When she walked into her son's room three days after surgery, Mary saw the little nurse look at the thermometer she held, the dark wings of her eyebrows moving closer together.

"How high is it?"

"It's been going up all day, Mrs. Soergel. We've put Scott on a specially controlled blanket. It's filled with water so that it can be either heated or cooled. It's like ice right now."

Mary repeated her question, "How high is it?" and her stomach lurched in fright at the quiet reply. "One hundred and six."

"He can't take that very long, can he?"

"No, he can't. I'm going to start giving him ice packs on his bare body right now, to try to bring it down."

"May I help?"

"Surely, if it would make you feel better to do something."

"It would."

"You wring out the towels then. I'll change them."

Mary sat by the window several hours later, looking out at the sky as the first star twinkled reassurance to her. "I feel like Scott looks," she thought.

The dark half-circles the eyelashes made on his face, now alabaster white, were the only spots of color. As his mother watched, his eyes opened. They looked very large and dark in the twilight haze as they peered out beyond her, widening suddenly.

"Look, Mother." He raised his hand, pointing out the window. "There is Jesus out there."

Startled, Mary jumped up and walked closer to the window. She looked across the U-shaped court to the windows opposite the one where she stood.

"No, Scott. Those are doctors over there. See, you can see them looking through the microscopes on the tables in front of them."

"No, Mother." He raised his hand again. Mary looked up in the sky. She saw only stars, bright pinpoints in the darkness.

Scott's face shone. "Mother! It is Jesus. See how he glows. His robe, Mother, how white it is. Oh, Mother!" Scott's voice fell to a whisper. "Jesus, Jesus."

Mary's heart began to pound. Scott's eyes closed. She walked back to the bedside and felt for Scott's pulse. It beat slow and steady against her finger.

Back in the apartment Mary found a note from Harry propped against the vase on the end of the buffet in the hall. "Gone to visit some friends in New York. Back in two or three days. Food in refrigerator. Eat it." She walked to the desk, picked up the phone, and dialed her home number without stopping to take off her coat.

Norm's voice brought her a little closer to reality. "We're all fine. I was just chewing the kids out when you called. I came home and Becca is still up. It's almost eleven o'clock. They didn't take back the overdue library books. The list of jobs I left for them isn't finished. I don't know what I have to do to get a little cooperation around here. You sure haven't taught them much about working, I can tell you that."

"Oh, why did I bother to call?" Mary asked desperately.

As Scott grew stronger, Mary's mind turned more often to the children she had left at home. She read and reread their letters as she traveled on the bus and subway.

Dear Mom,
    I'm glad you called last night. I wrote you a letter

Wednesday, and still haven't mailed it yet.

I wonder if Dad is paying the bills. I doubt if he is. Thank you for your postcards. It is very nice to get one from you every day. I got three A's on three algebra quizzes. By the way, I've gained weight. I weigh about 129-130. Pretty bad. I am determined to lose seven pounds. And I will. I promise you that by the time you get home, I will have lost seven pounds. *I promise.* (A little confidential buildup for me.)

I am listening to WRIT and they have some pretty good songs on. Dad is not home and I don't think he will be home at 10:30 like he said he would. In fact, I know he won't be home then. He never is home when he says he will be. Never. He is pretty mean sometimes and doesn't explain anything, so I don't know what is coming off. But I know he means well (I think) and try not to let it bother me, though sometimes it does. To tell the truth, most of the time it does.

Love,
Josh

Dear Mom,

Josh painted a real good picture on his canvas. The cats are getting big. How are you, and how is Scott? Ebbie is fine. Gram made Josh and me clean up the house. Gretch got to go out to play. Gram told me I can't climb trees. She says it is not ladylike. Last night Josh and I slept on the shelves in the spare closet. We used the old clothes in there for covers.

Dad is at work. He yelled at me and Josh because we climbed up the trapdoor into the attic. We found some old pictures of you. We read your high school yearbook. We were looking for some more pictures of you when Dad caught us. He yelled at us.

Everybody is bringing over casseroles and cookies and cakes and pies. Gram is keeping a list You

should see it. It's pages and pages. I've got to go and
wash the dishes.

Love,
Heidi

Mary smiled and read the letter from Gretchen.

Dear Mom,
   Gram went home for a couple of days. She said she
was rather tired. Josh and Heidi short-sheeted her
bed. I told them how to do it, but I really didn't think
they would. They are really acting bratty. When they
think Gram is going to tell them to do some work,
they hide. I know where their favorite hiding place
is—the spare closet.
   Becca really misses you. She always wants to sleep
with me. She follows me around and drags her blanket and sucks her thumb. I think Dad misses you too.
He is hardly ever home. When he is, he usually yells.
   I can't think of anything else to say. Say hi to Scott.

Love,
Gretch

P.S. This picture is for you from Becca. She said to
tell you it means, "Come home."
   P.S. again. Josh and Heidi were mad at me. They
chased me into your room, so I locked the door. They
tried to get me out by spraying starch under the
door. Then Josh went out on the roof and tried to
come in the window. He couldn't get it open. I had
locked it. Ha ha.

Mary jammed the letters down in her purse. She left the
room, walked to the elevator, and pushed the down button vigorously.
   "Why, yes, Mrs. Soergel." The receptionist looked surprised at the insistent note in the usually calm voice. "I'll
see if Dr. Crawford will see you."
   Mary leaned forward on the chair across from the doc-

tor's desk. "Dr. Crawford, Dr. Wepsic says Dr. Sweet is gone and can't be disturbed. He says he can't give permission for Scott to go home. He said the only thing that's keeping him here is the fact that the scar isn't healing because of the previous scar tissue that takes longer to heal. I know I can take care of changing that dressing at home. It might be days yet before it's healed. I have four other children at home. I want to get home to them."

The tall man with the soft eyes smiled at her. "I'm sure you do, Mrs. Soergel. I'll talk with Dr. Wepsic. You've been giving Scott the injection of pitressin, haven't you, for several days? You realize it's quite important that the urine be checked regularly so that the proper dosage is insured. You know how to do that also, I believe?"

"Yes. That's no problem. Scott's good about taking the shots. I'm sure we can manage."

"When do we eat?" As the plane flew westward Mary felt as if she were hearing a broken record. The question came frequently until the stewardess put down the tray in front of her son. Mary watched with amazement as he attacked the ice cream roll almost before the stewardess had released the sides of the tray, jabbing at the paper with the fork he had rolled out of the napkin. As she watched him devour all the items of food on the tray with ferocious intensity, Mary remembered Dr. Wepsic's final words.

"Scott's appetite may prove to be something of a problem. Experiments have been done on rats to study the effect of the removal of the hypothalamus gland on the appetite. The rats ate so much that they burst their own stomachs. One of our other patients woke up from the operating table demanding food. When he went home from the hospital, his mother gave him anything he wanted to eat. Now he's back in the hospital. He ate so much he couldn't carry the weight he gained so quickly. He broke his own hip eating."

She pushed the problem from her mind as the plane rolled to a stop, wanting to know what had been happening with the rest of her family since she had been gone.

Subtly the days began to expose the fact that Scott was not the same boy who had gone to Boston. His appetite began to dominate his life. It seemed slowly to gain control over the entire family as his weight began an inexorable climb upward. Monthly trips to Dr. Schumann with changes of appetite control medications did nothing to curb it.

As Scott grew fatter, his own attempts to control the situation became dramatic. The peanut butter jar had a sign taped to the lid: "Don't touch me, TNT inside." The cupboard shelves were labeled: "Danger, high explosives."

Norman and Mary began almost nightly battles over the situation, their voices as melodramatic as Scott's labels.

Norm: "You can't trust him."

Mary: "But he's always been so honest. Have you ever known him to lie?"

Norm: "You're damn right I've known him to lie. He's lying all the time about what he's eating. You refuse to face it, that's all."

Mary: "I refuse to face it! You act like it's his fault he's hungry. He can't help it."

Norm: "Of course he can help it. He could stop if he wanted. You can do anything you make up your mind to do."

Mary: "But you're making it worse yelling at him about it."

Norm: *"You're* sure not doing anything about it. All you do is baby him. Why don't you get tough with him?"

Mary: "You call it tough. I call it cruel."

Norm: "Sure. Blame me. It's all my fault."

The other children seemed to fade into the background. Scott started writing notes, putting up posters.

SELFISH SCOTT IS AT WORK
Mom, Dad, Josh, Gretch, Heidi, and Becca,
Please help me help myself. Food will be a threat as
long as I live. I must learn to overcome it. I can't just
pretend to hide from it!

Mary's ears became tuned in to Scott's midnight hours. He became a lone eater. She tried to sneak down to the kitchen before Norm was aware that Scott was sitting at the kitchen table with chocolate milk and a three-layer peanut butter and banana sandwich in front of him. Occasionally Mary was wakened by wild sounds from the direction of the kitchen. Norm, six-pack of beer in hand, and Scott, fortified with stacks of food in front of him, were as lethal a combination as any two wild animals. One night after such a confrontation, Scott came into the bedroom where his mother lay, pillow over her head to shut out the noise.

Tragedy clouded Scott's eyes. "Mother, does God love people who kill themselves?"

The next day Mary called Dr. Crawford. A week later Scott was back in Massachusetts General. Dr. Crawford wrote that they had put him in the metabolic research ward. The only food he saw was that served him in his own room. His weight started to go down. After he had lost thirty pounds, they sent him home, determined to start school in the fall.

"I hope Scott reads more when he goes to school." Mary sat across from her husband at the kitchen table. Norm was drinking beer as he read the evening paper.

"Oh, he will. He'll be all right when school starts again."

"You know the neuroophthalmologist said his vision was very poor."

"Sure. But you told me yourself Dr. Crawford proved him wrong. He showed him how Scott could read small print, in spite of the fact he tested 20/100."

"I know. But he never reads anymore. He used to read all the time."

"That's because he's always thinking about food." Norm picked up the carton and pulled out another can of beer. "He'll be all right when he gets back to school. Take his mind off food. Did anyone feed the dog today? I didn't see any food in his dish when I came through the garage."

Scott struggled to keep up with the abbreviated course that had been set up for him. He was placed in the honors courses he had qualified for before he went to Boston. Instead of diminishing, his appetite seemed to increase after school started. Mary stopped having any kind of dessert except fresh fruit. The level in the sugar jar went down. Nobody ever saw him eat any, but it seemed as if they were always out of sugar.

Josh walked into the kitchen one day as his mother was peeling potatoes for dinner. "Mother, do you want to know what those stupid kids are doing at school? They're throwing nickels on the floor in front of the candy machine. Then they stand and laugh when Scott gets down on his hands and knees to look for them."

"Oh, Josh." Mary put down the potato she held, shocked at the picture his words evoked. "Can't you do something about it?"

"What can I do about it? They wouldn't listen to me. It would only make it worse for him if I said something."

Mary sat at the kitchen table, a cup of coffee in front of her, watching the wind swirl the snow at the angle where the garage met the house. The force took the last few dried oak leaves from the big tree in front of the window. A tear slid from the corner of her right eye.

"I feel as if we're losing all our leaves too, God. What's happening to us? I don't have to tell you that Scott's schoolwork was too much for him, and that we had to let him drop out. You know that. I suppose you know all about what's happening with me and Norm too. I wish I did. Why isn't Norm ever home anymore? Why won't he talk to me when he is home? Why do we fight so much? How can he stand to sit in that dark, smelly old tavern with that bunch of derelicts?"

"Mother." Scott walked into the kitchen. "I just can't stand living like this. I want to find out what's wrong with me, why I fall asleep all the time, why I can't think straight."

"I'd like to find out too, Scott. I'll make an appointment with Dr. Schumann for the day after Christmas. We'll tell him everything that's been happening. Maybe he'll have some idea of what to do."

Scott's eyes were cloudy. "Good. I'm sick of going up there and feeling like he doesn't really want to know how I feel. I have to know. Let's do it now. I don't care about Christmas."

"I know you don't. But let's wait. It's only two weeks away. The last two Christmases have been so awful. It really doesn't seem fair to the rest of the family to mess this one up too."

The day after Christmas they left the clinic, walking down the side of the road in the sleet. Scott's face was red. He strode ahead of his mother with big steps, his feet thumping against the ground. He walked faster and faster. He raised his fists in the air. His voice shouted the words. "I want to know! I want to find out what's wrong with me! I can't find out! Nobody will tell me! Nobody will help me!"

"Scott! Scott!" Mary ran to catch up. She looked up at the junior high as they raced past and Scott continued to shout. "Don't make so much noise. Everybody will hear you."

"Good. I want everybody to hear me." His steps slowed, his voice softened. "I can't stand this, Mother.

Why won't that doctor talk to me? Why won't he listen to me when I try to tell him what's wrong?"

"I don't know, Scott. I'll write to Dr. Crawford in Boston as soon as we get home."

Mary was waiting for Norman to come home from work. She picked up the yellow spiral notebook she had bought at the grocery store. She tucked her leg under her and chewed on the end of her pencil, rereading what she had written.

> Dear Journal,
>
> I am a little past the age of most people who start a diary. I started a journal a while back, but I am afraid I neglected him. I'll try to do better with you. Maybe talking to you will help to get it all a little straightened out. Maybe I can look back and see what, and why, and whether.
>
> With Scott in the hospital, the rest of the kids have become life-size. They have voices that I can hear. I have a mind to listen when they talk to me. Norm and I are going to Boston to visit Scott the first week in March. Harry and bride have gone to Florida, so we will stay in their new apartment.
>
> March 3
> Dear Journal,
>
> I'm really glad that we came to Boston. Norm and I are discovering its charm together. It's so nice to share what I have enjoyed discovering all by myself. Yesterday we took Scott out for an excursion. The three of us visited the ship *Constitution*. Scott looks wonderful. He and Norm seem to be good friends again. Thank God.
>
> March 6
>
> I had a good conversation with Dr. Crawford today. It made me understand Norman's attitude to-

ward Scott. He explained that the fact that Norman had been such a good father before he found out Scott had a brain tumor made it all the more difficult to accept what had happened. He said before the time we knew he had a tumor, Scott had been realizing all the potential that Norman was never able to develop in himself because of his father's Huntington's disease. To have all of Scott's achievements suddenly snatched away by the fact of the brain tumor was more than Norm could handle. So when Scott has been seemingly destroying himself with the indulgence of his appetite, Norm has completely lost his cool.

I never thought of it like that. Thank God for Dr. Crawford. On leaving his office, I passed the young doctor who asked me if Norman had ever been examined for Huntington's disease. When I got back to Scott's room, it was empty. I sat and thought for a long time by myself. My mind was full of questions.

Why won't Norm talk about his father? Is it that he won't, or can't? He always says he can't remember. What would it be like to have a father you can't remember? Is this possible? Is the mind capable of shutting out so important a person as a father?

God, I wish I knew more, more about the human mind.

Is this why Norm sits in the tavern instead of coming home?

CHAPTER EIGHT

SAFE IN A COCOON

Mary sat at the lunch counter, coffee cup in her hand. She was trying to erase the two weeks that had elapsed since she had been in Boston with her husband; they had been such a dismal disappointment to her. Instead of the trip reestablishing the good relationship she had once had with Norm, communication seemed to have deteriorated since their return. She tried not to think about the night before when she had waited up in vain, then fallen into a fitful sleep when Norman did not come home. Her feelings in the night had verged on despair.

"Hi, Mary. Are you saving this empty stool?"

She looked up in surprise. "No, Dan. Sit down."

She had met the man who sat down next to her at the recent Lenten series at their mutual church. She had been struck by his fine-cut, almost feminine handsomeness when he had joined the church several months earlier. She knew he was a psychologist who worked in a clinic in Milwaukee. She did not think he was married, at least she had never seen him with a wife. He had joined the church alone.

The corners of his eyes crinkled as he smiled at her.

"What did you think of the Lenten series?"

"I really enjoyed it. It was a new concept to me, the idea that we are called on to be Christ to the world. It seemed presumptuous, almost blasphemous to me at first. But then, as the weeks went on, it became logical. Of course we have to be Christ to the world. There is nobody else to do his work, is there, Dan?"

He laughed at her enthusiasm. "Mary, I truly enjoyed talking with you those nights after we listened to the lecture and discussed what Nate Thorpe had brought out. I thought the first night that there was something different about you."

She thought of his words on the way home. They had talked for an hour over repeated refills of coffee. She had forgotten her worries about her husband.

A week later, they met again at the same lunch counter. Mary felt his hand on her shoulder as she sat alone, reading the menu over the top of the counter where the waitresses prepared the short orders. She was trying not to think of the argument that had begun in the middle of the night when Norman came to bed, his eyes suspiciously foggy.

"Hi, Dan."

"Hi yourself." Small drops of water huddled in the shadows of his curls, which refused the discipline of a short haircut, sneaking out in rebellious clusters.

"You look like you've been walking in the rain."

"I have. I walked across the parking lot from church. I've been talking to Charlie. He said you've been in Boston. How's Scott?"

"Oh, he's doing fine. I was just reading a letter from him that came this morning."

"Read it to me. I'd like to hear what he has to say about himself."

Mary reached in her purse. She pulled the folded paper from the envelope and began to read against the background of restaurant chatter.

"Dear Family:
I'm improving. I get bored more easily now. I need more action. I have been feeling great. All full of

pleasant lively thoughts about home. It won't be long now. I talked to Dr. Crawford today. He said he could get me home by June 12 with no trouble, as long as my weight cooperates. I'll make the weight cooperate or die trying. I don't think I'll have any trouble. The operation seems to have helped quite a bit. Nice! Still can't go whole hog, but I can eat enough to feel comfortable and still lose. I'll have grilled steak, tomatoes with dressing, garlic buttered French bread and butter pecan ice cream for a starter when I get home.

Love,
Scott

The corners of Dan's eyes crinkled as he smiled at her. "He sounds as if his attitude is very good."

"Yes. It always has been. He's a brave boy."

"Mary, I had an interesting talk with Charlie this morning. I've thought, ever since the Lenten series at church, that we should have some kind of weekly discussion similar to those nights. They seemed to stimulate so many people. What do you think of the idea?"

"I think it's a great one. I like it."

"Good. I made a date to talk with him again next Monday. Why don't you come too?"

"I'd love to, Dan, but I can't. I don't have a car."

"That's no problem. I'll pick you up. Eleven-thirty all right?"

Mary's mind was on that conversation at the lunch counter as she drove home after she bought the groceries. It troubled her in a way she couldn't understand.

"Foolish." Her mind scolded her. "You're letting your imagination run away with you." She remembered the way Dan had made her feel as he sat at the same table every week and provoked her brain to dig ever more deeply into her own responses and attitudes. "Like he was the robin, and I was the worm," she thought. "I didn't want to come up out of the safe, warm earth where I have lived all my life."

She was wondering if she could call Dan and cancel the date with Charlie as she scrubbed the kitchen early Monday morning. The phone rang when she had washed away about half the week's dirt.

"Mrs. Soergel, Dr. Crawford would like to speak with you."

After he had asked about the weather and the rest of the family, Dr. Crawford came to the reason for his call.

"We will be sending Scott home on Wednesday, Mrs. Soergel." He paused a moment. When he resumed the conversation, Mary had the feeling he was choosing his words very carefully. "Scott hasn't been feeling well this week. He had been making very satisfactory progress until about two weeks ago. His digestive system is functioning very well, very well indeed. His weight loss continues. He has been on a regular exercise schedule. He's regaining the muscular abilities which were impaired by his considerable weight gain. When he indicated that he wasn't feeling well, we ran him through a series of tests. They showed no abnormalities. We have repeated all the tests. We find nothing physiologically wrong with Scott."

"What do you mean, he isn't feeling well?"

"He's sleeping a considerable amount of the time. He says he thinks he has flu. He says he feels weak and dizzy."

"What do you think is causing it?"

"Mrs. Soergel, the psychiatrist and I have had a running battle about Scott right along. He has maintained that Scott has suffered too great a degree of brain damage to be able to function in the normal world. I have disagreed with him. I've disagreed most emphatically. Scott's symptoms right now, however, are caused by his emotions. He's hesitant to reenter the normal world; he feels safe and secure in the hospital, as in a cocoon." The line went dead. Mary jiggled the receiver, put her finger on the black, plastic bar, and pushed it up and down. There was no sound.

She knelt down by the scrub pail. She picked up the brush, swished the water around the floor in ever widening circles, trying to wash the doctor's words from her mind. Her stomach felt tightly knotted. The old feeling of cold dread had returned.

She stood at the window at 11:25, her mind a jumble of emotions. When she saw the black car pull into the driveway, she ran out the front door. Dan opened the door of the car. She slipped into the front seat beside him.

"What's the matter, Mary? You look worried."

She was unused to such quick perception of her feelings. She looked at the man in the seat beside her. The emotion she felt was apparent in her hazel eyes, now large and deeply troubled.

"Oh, Dan." She swallowed hard. "Oh, Dan."

"Mary, what is it? What's wrong?" The warm hand reached out to cover the clenched fist that was hitting at her lap. "Tell me."

Like a dam broken open by his sympathetic listening, Mary's words poured out on the way to the church. She talked rapidly, aware that she was exposing her feelings to him at a depth she had never revealed to any other person. But she was unable to shut off the flow of words. When the car stopped in front of the church, she couldn't remember just what she had said, but she felt strangely released. She blew her nose on the hanky he took from his shirt pocket.

"Mary, I want you to know that if there is anything, and I mean anything at all, that I can do to help you when Scott comes home, I want you to ask me. I want to help you, Mary."

As she stepped from the car, he held the door open for her. Her words surprised her. "You know, Dan, I think you can help. Yes, I think you can."

He put his arm around her shoulders. He squeezed re-assuringly.

Mary's mind was far from their conversation as Dan and Charlie discussed possible formats for a weekly sharing group.

Dan reminded her of the offer he had made when he brought her back home, and again in a phone call a week later.

"How is Scott, Mary?"

"He's really sick, Dan. He's been home almost a week. His face is white. He has shadows under his eyes. We went to church yesterday, just Scott and me. During the first few minutes, Scott whispered to me that he felt sick. He walked out. When he didn't come back, I went to find him. He was sitting on a chair in the basement, his head leaning against the wall. He said he felt all closed in and shaky. He said his heart was pounding. He threw up. We went home."

"What does Norman say?"

"Oh, he said it's probably the flu."

"Do you agree?"

"No, Dan. I think Dr. Crawford was right. I think he's afraid of the real world, full of healthy people."

"Mary, have you ever heard of the prayer group that meets at Swansons'?"

"Yes. I have a neighbor who told me about it. I met Karen and Jack Swanson when we were talking about open housing for Oconomowoc; in fact, they were here for a meeting about it. Why?"

"I've been involved in those prayer meetings since they started, Mary. We've prayed for people with serious problems. God has answered our prayers and healed people of some really serious conditions. Why don't you let me come and pray with Scott? I could come alone, or bring some other people with me. What do you say?"

Mary felt as if a chill wind was blowing through the

crack in the kitchen door near the phone. She shivered slightly. Her throat felt tight. She opened her mouth, then closed it again.

"Mary, are you there?"

"I don't know what to say, Dan. I'll think about it. I have to go now. Thanks for calling."

She recorded her feelings a few nights later in her journal.

> I don't know why the thought of Dan praying for Scott should scare me like it does. I haven't mentioned it to Norm. He hasn't been home enough to talk to him about Scott, or anything. I don't think he even knows how sick Scott feels. Scott is sleeping most of the time. His color is ashen grey. His eyes are dull and listless. He bears hardly any relationship to the boy he once was. He seems disinterested in everything and everybody. He doesn't even care about eating. I don't know if I should write to Dr. Crawford. What good would that do? I just don't know. Period.

Her mind was on the problem of Scott as she did the week's wash on Monday morning. She kicked around the thought of calling Dan Cardiff until her brain felt battered and confused. She spoke the words aloud as she carried the blue laundry basket up the stairs, holding it tightly against her tummy to ease the strain on her back.

"God, I don't know what to do. I don't know about calling Dan. I surely would like to. He might be able to help us. At least he would talk to me about Scott. But I don't know, God. I just don't know. I don't know how that would make Norman feel, so I'm not going to call him. If you want him to pray for Scott, you send him. I'm going to leave the matter entirely up to you. Thank you, God."

It was Friday morning. Mary was ironing in the upstairs hall when she heard the dog bark, signaling a caller at the front door.

"Oh, no!" she muttered under her breath as she ran down the stairs. "I thought for once I was going to get caught up on the ironing."

She saw the slim figure of Dan Cardiff on the cement doorstep. There was an uncertain note in the usually confident voice. "Mary, I just really can't explain why I'm here. I was driving in to the clinic. In fact, I was almost there. It seemed to me the Lord was telling me to come back and see Scott. Is he up?"

Mary held open the screen door. "Yes, come on in, Dan. Scott just went downtown with his dad. They said they would be right back." She walked ahead of him into the living room. "Sit down."

Mary sat down on the couch, tucking her legs under her. The big red dog investigated the unfamiliar legs as Dan sat down. Eb's tail began to wag. He slumped in a sudden heap at the feet of the man in the grey chair.

"Well, you're accepted." Mary smiled as Dan leaned over to pat the dog with long, smooth strokes along his back. He looked up, his eyes suddenly serious.

"How's Scott, Mary?"

"He's sick. He's really sick."

Dan reached inside his coat and pulled out a small book. The cover spoke of an easy familiarity, with slight lines worn on its blue leather surface. "Do you know what this book is?"

"Why, a Bible."

Dan held the book in front of him and tapped its cover with the fingers of his left hand. His eyebrows moved closer. The light in his eyes seemed to spark into hers as he said, "It's more than a Bible. It's the Word of God. The Word of God, Mary. Do you believe that?"

Mary was startled by his intensity. "I guess I do."

"Mary, I said believe. Believe. To guess is not to believe. Do you really believe that this is God's holy Word?"

Mary's chin went up. Her back straightened. Her tone was slightly haughty. "Of course I do."

"Good. That's all I need to know. Then hear what God has to say about Scott." He leafed through the pages quickly. "There are hundreds of passages that could apply to his situation. Here." His finger stopped. "John, chapter eleven, when Jesus heard that Lazarus was ill. He said, 'This illness is not unto death; it is for the glory of God, so that the Son of God may be glorified.' Think of that, Mary. Scott's illness could glorify God."

He didn't notice the frown that creased her forehead. He continued to search the Scriptures. "Here. Matthew 10:8. Jesus was charging the disciples. He said, 'Heal the sick, raise the dead, cleanse lepers, cast out demons. You receive without pay, give without pay.'" He turned back a page. "Matthew 8:14—'And when Jesus entered Peter's house, he saw his mother-in-law lying sick with a fever. He touched her hand, and the fever left her, and she rose and served him. That evening they brought to him many who were possessed with demons, and he cast out the spirits with a word.' Just think, Mary." Dan's blue eyes gleamed when he looked up at her. "With a word. 'And healed all who were sick. This was to fulfill what was spoken by the prophet Isaiah, He took our infirmities and bore our diseases.'"

Dan closed the Bible with a snap. "Mary, the great tragedy of our churches is that they have turned their back on the Christ, the Messiah. They are teaching instead only Jesus the man. Sure, he was a wonderful person, the finest man who ever lived; but Mary, he was so much more than that. He *is* so much more than that. He can still do all of those things today—heal the sick, cast out demons, take our infirmities, and bear our diseases, but we won't let him." He shook his head. His voice fell to a whisper. "We won't let him—because we don't really believe he can."

Dan placed his hand on Mary's arm. "Mary, won't you let Christ heal Scott?"

The blue eyes seemed to have captured hers. She tried to look away from them but they held her firmly with their piercing light. She shook off his hand, got up from the couch, walking away from him. She turned her back for a moment and stood very still. He rose and followed her. He stood closely in front of her. His proximity forced her to look up at him.

"I don't know, Dan. This scares me."

"Mary, why should it scare you?"

"I don't know. It just does."

He reached out for her hand. He placed it on the Bible. His hand was warm on top of hers. "Mary, this book, this little worn-out book contains all the faith you need. It contains all of God's promises. It is the substance of things hoped for, the evidence of things unseen that the Book of Hebrews speaks about. It says, 'God is not a man that he could lie.' Mary, Jesus is either a liar or he can heal Scott. It is as simple as that. Take your choice."

Mary drew her hand away. She walked a few steps away from him. "I don't know, Dan. I'll have to think about this."

He put the book back into his pocket. "Well, you think about it. I'd better go."

"But aren't you going to stay and see Scott?"

"No." He walked toward the front door, the big dog at his heels. "I'll be back."

Mary watched him walk down the brick walk in front of the house. He turned when he was almost to his car. He raised his hand in a quick wave, turned, and opened the door of the car. She watched the black car drive down the road until only a small dust cloud remained. She went back into the living room and sat down on the couch. She leaned back. She stretched out her legs and put her head on the back of the couch.

"God," she whispered, "I don't know. Why am I so

scared? I've gone to church all my life. You know that. Charlie is the best minister I've ever known. He never talks like that." She stood up, started walking back up-stairs to her ironing. "No, God. You're going to have to show me more. I'm scared."

CHAPTER NINE

"PRAYER CHANGED MY LIFE"

Mary stood at the kitchen sink the next morning. She scrubbed hard at the breakfast dishes, trying to erase the questions that were in her mind. Where had Norman been until two in the morning? She had sat up waiting, wanting to tell him about Dan's visit.

"Hi, Mare." Her husband's voice caught her unawares as he walked into the kitchen. He came up behind her and put his arms around her, pinning her arms to her sides with a squeeze. She broke his hold with a quick jab of her elbows. She turned around, then leaned back against the sink, looking up at him, wiping her hands on her apron. "What time did you tie up at work last night?"

"That's right. What time did you tie up?" The voice was high and mocking. Mary's hazel eyes shot sparks at the dark brown ones as his brows knotted together. His finger pointed in her face. "I'd like to ask you a few questions for a change. Where in the hell are all my T-shirts? I never have any T-shirts around this damn place. All I ever get is questions or gloomy looks. If you can't get the work done, why don't you get one of those lazy daughters to do something? I'm tired of being the only one who ever does anything around this house ... it's falling apart!"

Mary's lips clamped together. As his voice stopped, she shot out the breath she had been holding with a deep hissing sigh. She walked to the basement stairway with quick, hard steps. She grabbed the jacket that hung inside the door.

"Where do you think you're going?"

She whirled around. "I'm going down to get some food for your children. How do you think I can shop for groceries when our only car is always sitting outside some tavern?"

"Why shouldn't I go to a tavern when my house is always a mess and I never have any T-shirts in my drawer? And what about socks? Where in the hell are all my socks?"

Mary held out her hand. "May I have some money, please?"

"And that's another thing. What happens to all the money I give you? You never have any money. What do you do with all of the money I give you? You don't know, do you? You never know what you do with a damn thing, do you?"

"Well, I do know I don't spend it over a bar. I know I don't spend it on clothes for myself. I haven't had a new winter coat since Josh was a baby. That's quite a few years, wouldn't you say?"

He reached in his pocket and pulled out a roll of bills. He threw one at her. "Go to hell."

Mary grunted in anger as she stooped over to pick up the money off the floor. She slammed the door hard as she ran out and down the front walk.

"Oh, Mary, are you leaving?"

Mary looked blankly at the smiling face that spoke to her through the open window of the big, black car parked in the drive. The woman spoke with a Southern accent.

"No, you don't know me, but my Carol has grown very fond of your Gretchen. Perhaps Gretchen has mentioned her to you. They met at the beach a few weeks ago. We're new in town. We recently moved from Arizona. I'm Mrs. Goodman."

"Oh, yes, she did. Does your daughter play the piano?"

"Yes. She's an excellent pianist. We're very proud of her. But that's not what I came to talk with you about. Do you have a moment, or do you have to go somewhere right away?"

"No." Mary turned back down the walk as the dark-haired lady opened the door and joined her. "I was just going to get a few groceries. It can wait."

Norm's yellow-robed back was going through the door into the kitchen as they walked into the living room.

"Norm, this is Mrs. Goodman. They've just moved here from Arizona." Norm nodded at the visitor and continued on into the next room.

Mrs. Goodman sat on the chair nearest the door, under the picture of Christ that hung on the wall. Her dark eyes looked directly into Mary's as she leaned over, handing her the book she held in her hand. "Here," she said, "I brought you this book. It's by Dr. Francis Parker."

Mary took the book and looked at the words on the paper cover, *Prayer Can Change Your Life*. She looked across at her attractive caller.

"Prayer *can* change your life, Mary. It changed mine."

Mary forgot the earlier moments of conflict as the story her visitor began to tell caught her interest. Mrs. Goodman told a fascinating tale of ulcers healed, houses purchased; of moving from state to state as if Jesus Christ had drawn the blueprint, and all she and her husband had to do was follow it.

"And, Mary," she concluded, "there is a prayer group here just like the one we left in Arizona. It meets at a very lovely home on the lake. I've just come from a Bible study that's held there every Wednesday morning. We prayed for Scott this morning. We prayed for him last week too. That's why I'm here, Mary. I want to invite you to go with my husband and me this Friday evening."

Startled, Mary asked, "Is that the group that Dan Cardiff spoke to me about?"

"Dan is very active in our group. He's one of the people who organized it. So you know Dan. Isn't that interesting?"

"I don't know him very well."

"Mary, why don't you come to the meeting Friday evening and see for yourself? My husband and I would be glad to pick you up."

Mary caught her top lip between her teeth. She jiggled her left leg, as if her thoughts disturbed it. She let her breath out in a big sigh as she looked up at her guest. "OK."

Mrs. Goodman smiled broadly as she got up from her chair, and leaned over to pick up her purse. She stood still for a moment. Then, as if she had a change of mind, she sat down again, balancing her purse on her knee. She looked at Mary. The brown eyes that had shone with excitement as she had talked looked suddenly guarded, hiding the question in them with a dull curtain of doubt.

Mary had to suppress a smile at the drama in the voice as it lowered almost to a whisper and breathed, "At these meetings at Swansons', they speak in tongues."

Listening to her visitor, Mary had forgotten her anger with her husband. After Mrs. Goodman left, she went into the kitchen. Norman was drinking coffee and reading a magazine.

"Norm, did you hear what that woman was saying?"

Her husband looked up from his magazine.

"No, what was that woman saying?"

Mary sat down opposite her husband. "She was telling me all the things prayer has done in her life. She asked me to go to a prayer meeting with her and her husband Friday night. She wondered if you would like to go too."

Norman reached over to turn up the radio as the announcer gave the weather report. Mary waited until the music came in.

"I think I'll go, Norm. They've been praying for Scott. Do you want to go too?"

"No. I don't want to go. But you go pray. Maybe it will help you keep some T-shirts in my drawer."

Friday night the sun was setting over the lake as they drove down the long driveway. Mary caught her breath at the beauty she saw when the car rounded the curve, then crossed the bridge that covered the stream leading from the lake to the moat surrounding the small island. The house at the top of the hill seemed as if it should be described in a romantic historical novel dealing with the turn of the century, Mary's imagination said as she looked at the blue slate roof that covered the long three-storied white house with curving bay windows and round cupolas.

Mary sat in the semi-circle of worshipers on the large porch at the front of the house, overlooking the lake. She watched the celebration of the sunset as the red dimmed into orange and then a soft gold just beyond the horizon. The smooth surface of the lake reflected the spectrum of colors. The gull that glided over the water seemed to lead her back into her childhood.

She pictured a big room in a meeting hall in Minnesota, where the chubby little girl sat in the front row of a large group of singers, swinging her legs in time to the music. Her father, state president of the Christian Endeavor Society, led the singing with the powerful baritone voice that had supported every church choir she had ever participated in.

Mary looked at the man who had been introduced to her as Andy. He played the piano, his hands ranging skillfully up and down the keyboard, drawing music from the people as well as from the instrument he played. Mary looked past Andy to where Dan sat at the far side of the room. His head was bowed, as if he were praying. His eyes were closed. Mary felt warm and protected.

The next morning the coffee shop was busy with the usual Saturday morning chatter.

"Hi, Mary." Dan's voice surprised her. "What are you up to this morning?"

"Eavesdropping." She looked up at the blue eyes smiling down at her. "I'm a compulsive eavesdropper."

"Shame on you. I was certainly glad to see you at the meeting last night. What did you think of it?"

"It was interesting."

"Let's go sit in a booth." He picked up her coffee, reaching for her check. Mary slid into the booth across from him.

"Tell me how the meeting made you feel, Mary."

"It made me feel like the nursery school children I teach."

"What do you mean, Mary?"

"I don't know. When I heard that man speak in tongues, I just felt like I do when a three-year-old looks at me."

"Ummm," Dan mused. "Maybe that's not so bad— 'except that ye be as little children.' How would you like to have the gift of tongues?"

"I wouldn't."

"Why not?"

"I don't know. Why should I want it?"

"Because it is a gift from God. Our Father who loves us can only give us good gifts that we need. So why shouldn't we accept them?"

"But what good is it if nobody can understand it?"

"Didn't you hear the interpretation in the meeting? The one who interprets the gift understands it. God gives him the words."

"I wouldn't trust myself to do that. I might just be making up something that sounded good. How would I know it wasn't just my own mind?"

"But, Mary, the Bible says the gift of tongues is for our own edification. Thrnk of it, God can give you a language just to talk to him, just between the two of you. You don't have to use it in a meeting. I never have. I just pray to God with my gift of tongues. I use it every day."

"I pray every day too," her voice interrupted his.

"I don't mean to argue with you about this, Mary. It is just so new to you. I hope you keep coming to the meetings. Do you know what these meetings are to me?" He answered her raised eyebrows, "An answer to what I've been looking for all my life."

He looked at her in silence for a minute. His memory took charge of his eyes. He seemed not to see a rather tired-looking mother whose rumpled hair was beginning to show tinges of grey, but the little boy he had been.

"When I was thirteen and fourteen, I spent hours, days, trying to decide if I should become a priest. Half of me wanted desperately to say yes, the other half said no.

"Why did half say no, Dan?"

"I think because of what the church never did for my mother. My mother was a very devout Catholic. She went to mass every morning of her life. She was a real saint." His voice lowered. He shook his head. "She was also a fool."

Mary didn't know what to say. Her fingers creased fanfolds in the white napkin as she waited for him to continue.

"I'm the second of thirteen children. My father was an alcoholic. In those days we called them 'drunks.' I know now that he was a sick man. When I was young, all I knew was that we never had enough food. But he always found enough cash to buy a bottle."

"Is that why you're a marriage counselor?"

He smiled at her quick perception. "Probably. Partly, at least. But you can be sure I never try to counsel a marriage where alcoholism is involved. That would be as stupid as if I tried to stop the bleeding if somebody was dying of cancer."

"What do you do with alcoholics?"

"I refer them to the man in our clinic who is trained to help alcoholic families. He's a Catholic priest, one of my best friends. He's fantastic." He looked across the booth with a shake of his head. "You're too good a listener. I didn't want to talk about me and my work. I want to talk about you."

"Dan, what did you mean when you said, 'These meetings are the answer to what I've been looking for all my life'?"

"OK." He smiled at her. He reached inside his coat and pulled out his wallet. He opened it up, feeling with his index finger in the flap, and pulled out a piece of paper, creased, folded, worn thin.

"When I was searching for my vocation in my early teens, I found this quotation by Michael Ramsey who was then Archbishop of Canterbury. I knew if I could find what he had described, I would have the answers." His voice deepened as he read. "'The world can be saved by one thing only, and that is worship. For to worship is to quicken the conscience by the holiness of God, to feed the mind with the truth of God, to purge the imagination by the beauty of God, to open the heart to the love of God, to devote the will to the purpose of God.' Dr. Ramsey says here the same thing de Chardin meant when he said, 'The day is not far distant when humanity will realize that biologically it is faced with a choice between suicide and adoration.' "

"Do you mean that you have found how to worship, to adore?"

"Yes, Mary." A smile again lit his face. "In the charismatic worship I have discovered the presence of God."

"Doesn't *charisma* mean 'gifts?' "

"Yes, that's right. In the charismatic worship service, we worship using all the gifts God has offered to us."

Mary folded the white paper fan in half. "Dan, you know that little woman that asked for prayer toward the end of the meeting?"

"Do you mean Ella, the one who said she and her husband were starting a camp for the inner city kids from Milwaukee?"

"Yes, that's the one. Was she serious? Are they actually planning on going ahead on Monday with only $20 and 2,000 pounds of leather?"

"Absolutely. That's what's called 'living by faith.' "

"I guess." Mary's tone was questioning. "Do you think that's possible?"

"Sure I do. Do you know what I thought about when she asked for prayer? Didn't you tell me Scott knows quite a bit about working with leather?"

"Yes. Why?"

"I'm going up to the camp when it opens Monday. Why don't I stop and take Scott up with me? Maybe he could help. That might be the best thing in the world for Scott, if he could feel he were useful in helping someone else less fortunate than he is."

Mary busied herself picking up the house after Dan drove off with Scott Monday morning.

"Why are you singing, Mother?"

Mary looked in surprise at the sleepy-eyed girl with the tousled hair. "I don't know, Gretch." She hugged the warm body that leaned against her side. "Haven't you ever heard me sing before?"

Gretchen shook her head. "Not in the morning."

"I just feel like singing, I guess. What do you think it would be fun to do today? The boys are gone. Let's you and me and Heidi and Becca do something."

That evening she put her arms around her husband's neck as he walked through the kitchen door. He lifted her off the floor with a tight squeeze. He set her down, kissing her firmly. The dark brown eyes looked quizzically into her face, his brow creasing slightly, "Well, well. What's with you? What did you do that you shouldn't?"

"What do you mean, 'What did I do that I shouldn't?' " Her voice was indignant. "I went for a picnic back by the river with your daughters. That's what I did."

"Good. Where are the boys?"

"Josh is out on his bike somewhere. Scott went for a ride with Dan Cardiff, up to that camp I was telling you about."

"What camp?"

"You know. The one those people from the meeting the other night are trying to start for the kids from the inner city."

"Who did you say he went with?"

"Dan. Dan Cardiff. You know. He goes to our church."

"I don't remember him. What does he have to do with this camp?"

"I don't know. He said he was taking something up to them. He didn't say what. He thought maybe Scott could start some leather projects for the campers. What do you think?"

"All right with me. Where are the girls now?"

"Outside somewhere." She tried to pull away from his asking arms.

"Norm, no. Not now. The girls will be coming in any minute."

She started to laugh softly. He pulled her close, trying to persuade her with gentle nibbles on her neck. She saw the black car pull into the driveway. She pushed him away and walked to the window, waving at Dan as he backed out and drove down the road.

Norman walked to the refrigerator. He took out a can of beer. He jabbed the top with the point of the opener.

Scott's eyes shone as he walked into the kitchen. "Hi, Dad. Hi, Mom. Boy, that camp is really something. Is it all right if I go up there every day and teach the campers something about leather, Mother?"

He looked at his mother. She looked at his father. Neither one answered his question.

"I told them I would. They have all that beautiful leather. Nobody knows a thing about how to use it."

"But, Scott, that's pretty far. How would you get there?"

"Dan said he would pick me up tomorrow. Ella said Brian Steinke would be coming through here every day. He's a coach. He's going to teach swimming. She said they could use Josh to be a lifesaver. None of them swim really well."

"What do you think, Norman?"

He shrugged his shoulders. "I don't care. It's up to you."

"Is there a place you can rest if you get tired, Scott?"

"Sure, Mom. There are lots of beds."

Scott looked at his father. "I'm sure glad that you taught us how to camp, Dad. None of those kids know one thing about it."

Mary came out of the basement late the next afternoon as the boys walked in the back door. Scott's face was red. He slumped into a chair just inside the door. "I don't know, Mom. Those kids are animals. They're just like wild animals. You put a tool down, somebody grabs it. One kid tried to hit another over the head with a wrench. They can't do one thing without fighting. I don't know if I even want to go back." His voice sounded weak and tired.

"How did you do, Josh?" Mary looked at the boy standing in front of the refrigerator pouring orange juice into a glass.

The dark eyes smiled at her across the room. "Oh, if they got rough, I just picked them up and held them up-side down."

Mary's tone was matter of fact. "Why don't you give it at least one more day, Scott? It's supposed to be cooler to-morrow. It was probably partly the awful heat today, don't you think?"

The next evening Scott ran into the living room where his mother sat with Becca on her lap, a book in her hand. "Mother, it was a miracle, a real miracle. Those were changed kids. They couldn't have been nicer. They said 'please' and 'thank you.' They were so much kinder to one another. Before I went to lunch, I told them how happy I was about the way they were acting. After we had our dessert, Brian told them there would be twenty minutes to do whatever they wanted. What do you think they did?"

"I can't imagine, Scott. What did they do?"

"They pounded on the table and said, 'We want Scott, we want Scott,' so I gave them a little talk."

Curiosity sparked in her eyes. "What did you say?"

"Oh, I just said I thought it was God's plan that we should be learning to work together. I saw the salt and pepper shakers on the table in front of me, so I picked them up and sprinkled some in my hand. I said, 'See, the salt is white, the pepper is black. When you put them both on the food, the food tastes better. That's why God gave them both to us.' That's the way he wants his world to be, I told them. I said we were different colors, but God needs us both to make the world tastier for him. Then I said a little prayer. I thanked God for giving us this camping experience. I thanked him for the people who made it possible, for the river to fish in and the trees to climb. I thanked him for the craft house and the porch to eat on and the diamond to play baseball and the swimming pool." Scott looked across at his mother who sat with her arms around the little girl in her lap. "Mother, I thank God that he sent Dan to take me to Cross Acres."

Mary nodded her head. She rested her chin on top of Becca's soft hair. She remembered the feelings of uneasiness she had felt when Dan sat in the living room and talked excitedly about faith in action. She watched her husband as he put a match to the cigarette he held between his lips, shook it out, then dropped it in the ashtray. Scott looked at his father as Mary waited for him to say something about what Scott had shared with them. Norm reached for the newspaper on the shelf behind him, opened it, and began to read.

CHAPTER TEN

HUNTINGTON'S HITS HOME

After the children were tucked in bed, Mary walked up to where her husband sat. She held out a blue envelope. "We got a letter from Gayle. Do you want to read it?"

"You tell me what she said."

Mary sighed. "They're coming east in two weeks. They want to stop and visit us."

"Well, what's the matter with that?"

"I didn't say there was anything the matter with it. I simply said they were coming."

Norman rattled the newspaper he held, as if to shake off a pesky fly.

Mary persisted. "Gayle didn't say one word about how Ed is feeling. I feel ashamed for never answering the questions she asked me in that letter so long ago. Do you remember when she was wondering about Huntington's disease?"

Norm nodded. He didn't look up from the paper.

"Maybe we should help her find a good neurologist while they are here. What do you think?"

"Maybe." Norm picked up his paper and walked out into the kitchen. Mary heard him open the door of the refrigerator. She heard the defiant "pop" as he opened the can of beer. She walked up the stairs and went to bed.

The night the Ed Soergels arrived was a painful one. They were at the supper table when they heard a knock on the back door. When Mary answered, she saw her sister-in-law on the back steps. Gayle's tanned face had a frantic expression. Her blonde hair was windblown.

"Norm, come quick. Ed started to turn in the old drive-way in the back and jackknifed the trailer. The road is blocked."

Standing beside her brother-in-law, Mary was thankful that Norman had the trailer to divert him. Ed was unable to stand still. His knees jerked, as if a puppeteer had a string attached to each leg. His elbows moved in circular motions. His shoulders attempted to follow his head as it jutted the chin from side to side, giving up every so often, flopping the arms in rag doll limpness. Mary concentrated to understand the words that blurred with the movements of his tongue. He had grown thin. His face was lined and looked much older than his thirty-eight years.

Mary's stomach felt tight as they sat around the table after Norm pulled the trailer into a spot behind the house. They talked of the trip, the weather, everything but the reason for the change in Edwin. Mary looked across the table at her husband. She wondered if she were hiding her emotions as well as he was. She felt like lying down on the floor and crying. She wanted to go over to Edwin and put her arms around him and say, "I'm sorry." Instead she said, "More coffee, Norm?"

He got up from the table. "No, thanks." He walked to the refrigerator. "Want a beer, Ed?"

The first week of the visit passed quickly. Nobody men-tioned the changes in Edwin.

Mary felt as if they were walking through the lines writ-ten by a sick playwright. The whole week felt unreal to her. Instead of putting her arms around Ed and saying "I'm sorry," she did the same as everyone else—she treated him as if he were perfectly normal.

It was only after she was in bed that the actuality hit her. It was then that she remembered Edwin as he had been. She remembered the summer he had lived with them when he was in college. She recalled the way he had looked as he put his track shoes on every night and ran a mile to the golf course and a mile back before eating supper. She remembered how proud they had been watching him throw the pass that broke the passing record at Eastern Illinois. She saw, in her mind, how his teammates clustered around him and beat him on the back after he had run eighty yards for a touchdown, how his hips had swiveled from side to side as he outmaneuvered the opposition.

She saw in her mind's eye the headlines in the scrapbook his sister Shirlee had kept all the years he played football. What a contrast between that strapping athlete whose picture was pasted in that scrapbook and the man who was staying in her house!

Where there had been magnificent coordination, there was spasmodic motion, a series of jerks and swayings that defied description.

If the bright mind was still facile, it was disguised by the inability to communicate, the difficulties in articulation.

Only the disposition was the same, sweet and amenable. Only his eyes displayed the frustration he felt.

Mary spent the week fuming inwardly at her husband's refusal to discuss his brother's condition, his apparent endless hours of work. She determined to talk to Gayle the first chance she had to be alone with her. It came on Thursday.

"Gayle," she questioned as they sat in the empty house having a cup of coffee, "do you think Ed would go to a doctor while you are here?"

"No, Mary. I know he wouldn't."

"Why don't I try to make an appointment with Ben Schumann? He's really good. He found Scott's brain tumor. They were very impressed at Massachusetts General with that. I'll go see him with you if you want me to. I know he could help us decide what to do."

Mary hung up the phone.

"Good. Tomorrow at three. Norm will be home."

They planned a fun-filled morning. They went, without children, for a ride and picked up rye bread, sausage, cheese, and beer, then had a leisurely picnic by the river. Nobody mentioned the doctor's appointment. When they got home, Ed went upstairs. Gayle followed him.

Mary looked at the clock, saw it was one hour until they had to be at the doctor's office. She looked at her husband. He was standing with the refrigerator door open when they heard the shout from upstairs.

"No. I won't go. I won't go to any doctor."

Norman closed the refrigerator door and walked out of the kitchen. Mary followed. Norm walked up the stairs and to the door of the bedroom. Ed stood in the middle of the room, yelling at his wife. Gayle was sitting on the floor, her arm on the windowsill, her head down on her arm. Sobs shook her small body. Mary's eyes filled with tears. She walked from the room as she heard her husband say, "It won't hurt to go to a doctor, Ed. Mary and I will go with you and Gayle."

Dr. Schumann talked with them as Edwin was getting dressed. His voice was devoid of expression.

"Edwin does manifest symptoms of Huntington's disease, but I would like you to see a neurologist friend of mine in Milwaukee tomorrow to be sure."

The next night Mary sat waiting for Norman to come home from work. She had gone in with Gayle and Edwin to see the neurologist. Her mind felt crushed. When Norman walked in the back door, he looked at his wife. Mary sat at the kitchen table, trying to concentrate on the newspaper, to keep from hearing the question that had been repeating itself over and over in her head—"How am I going to tell Norman?" His first words were no help.

"Anything in the mail?"

"No. Were you expecting something?"

"No. Did anyone feed the dog?"

"Heidi did. She feeds him every day."

Norman walked over to the refrigerator.

"Where is everybody?"

"In bed. I was just waiting up for you."

Norm looked at her over the top of the refrigerator door. "Is this all the beer we have? I brought home a six-pack last night."

"Ed drank a couple before he went to bed. I think he was pretty upset."

Norm took the peanut butter jar from the cupboard shelf. He tore a paper towel off the roll on the wall, spread it on the table. He sat down, looking across the table at his wife, who was watching the circle the tea made as she swirled it around in her cup.

"What was he upset about?"

Mary watched her husband spread peanut butter on a square of cracker. He looked up at her, the question repeated in his eyes.

"The neurologist told him he was sure he had Huntington's."

Norman picked up the can opener. He speared two holes in the top of the beer can. Mary watched the foam gurgle out and down the side of the container. She took a deep breath.

"Norm, he said we should bring all of our kids in for an examination. He said they have a fifty percent chance of getting Huntington's disease by the time they're thirty."

Norm's head went down, his arm shot out across the top of the table in a sweeping curve as his neck arched back, as if he felt a blow to the belly.

He got up and ran into the bathroom. Stunned by this reaction, Mary watched the beer trickle off the tabletop in a widening puddle. She heard the plopping sounds of vomit. The retching stopped. Norm came swiftly through the kitchen.

"Where are you going?"

The only answer she heard was the slam of the door.

Gretchen and Heidi, curled close together in the bottom bunk, stirred as she climbed the ladder to flop onto the bed above them. She put her head under the pillow and tried to pray. "O God, O God, O God." The words continued as her body shook with her effort to restrain the shriek she felt rising from deep within her.

She began to feel as if she had been raised up above the bed. She floated effortlessly. From her mouth came faint syllables. She didn't recognize their meaning, but she couldn't control the flow. Anguish washed out of her as the new language poured out of her mouth in a steady stream.

The morning sun shining into the top bunk wakened her. She felt strangely peaceful. She crept down the ladder past her sleeping daughters. The snores that came from behind the bedroom door beside the bookcase told her that Norman was home. She pulled out the Bible, sat down on the floor, and leaned against the wall as she searched for some meaning to what she had experienced the night before. She stopped at Romans 8:26—"Likewise the Spirit helps us in our weakness; for we do not know how to pray as we ought, but the Spirit himself intercedes for us with sighs too deep for words. And he who searches the hearts of men knows what is the mind of the Spirit, because the Spirit intercedes for the saints according to the will of God."

CHAPTER ELEVEN

REPRIEVE

"Welcome home, Mary." Dan opened the door of the car. "How was the vacation? Are you glad to be home?"

"Yes and no." Mary smiled over at the man who steered out of the driveway. "I'm really glad to be going to a prayer meeting. I've missed them terribly. But I wasn't a bit happy to leave the wilderness. It was so beautiful. It was just like being in heaven. Remember that delightful island I told you about that we found at the end of our trip last year? This time we headed right for it. We had two canoes. Paddling along, it was the most exciting feeling, wondering if it was still there and just as beautiful as we remembered it."

Dan smiled at the enthusiasm in her voice. "And was it?"

"It was."

"How's Norm?"

"Wonderful. Norm is just the man to be with if you want to live on an island. He's so resourceful. He's at his best when he's camping. We all get along best when we camp. We work together. We always have. No fights, no problems getting anybody to work. Everybody pitches in."

"I've wondered what you do all day when you camp."

"There's lots to do. You have to gather wood to keep the campfire going. You have to pump your water and heat it over the campfire. We spend a lot of time cooking. We make pies and cakes and even bake bread."

"Sounds like a lot of work to me."

"Oh, it is work. But the work is fun. Even doing dishes is fun. You stand behind the picnic table and look out on the water. It's so still and peaceful. I can't explain or describe it so you would know how it really is."

Mary watched the trees as they drove, searching for the right words. "Every time I'm out in the wilderness, I think if I had only a few months to live, I'd want to spend it right there. You should have seen it when we left. The kids had the whole island decorated. They dug up wild flowers and ferns and weeds and made little flower beds all over the campgrounds. When they were little, a long time ago, we camped by a huge hollow stump. We lined it with moss and planted flowers in it. It was a sort of game we played, to keep it watered, to keep the flowers living. Every time we went for a walk in the woods, we brought back another plant for our stump. We've been doing it ever since, wherever we camp. This time Gretchen found a little log with a natural bowl in it. Josh jammed it between two birch trees. They lined the bowl with moss, and planted ivy in it, to hang down. The kids made a climbing maze on the end of the island over a big cliff that goes straight down into the water. They lashed logs between a little stand of birch trees, at different heights. They looked like monkeys swinging out over the cliff, hanging by their knees.

"How did Scott do?"

"Oh, he had a grand time. Do you know what we did this year that we've never done before? We had worship services every night, just as the sun was going down. We sat on the cliff beside the water. Everybody took turns giving a little message."

"Norm too?"

"Norm too. We always sang a song and read a Psalm, and Dan—do you know what?"

"No, Mary, what?" The blue eyes smiled.

"You know what that neurologist told me, that some of our kids have a fifty percent chance of having Huntington's disease before they reach the age of thirty?"

"What about it?"

"I took that book by Dr. Francis Parker, *Prayer Can Change Your Life*. I read it the first few days we were there. I thought about it a lot. Most of the time, in fact. Then on the first Tuesday we were camping—I remember for sure it was a Tuesday because I felt so different—I just felt a strange sense of peace. I forgot all about worrying about the kids getting Huntington's disease. And then when we got home, there was a letter from Dr. Crawford."

"I suppose you're going to tell me he wrote it on that same Tuesday. I know you're going to say he told you your kids would not get Huntington's disease."

"Exactly." Her voice had a note of surprise. "How did you know?"

"Norm doesn't show any signs of the disease, does he?"

"No. Not one. He's well past the dangerous age. I'm sure he won't get it." Her eyebrows knotted. "Why do you suppose that neurologist told me such a dumb thing, Dan?"

"I don't know, Mary. Doctors are people. They make mistakes just like all the rest of us. I'm afraid we tend to think of ministers and doctors as more than human."

Dan turned off the ignition. He held out his hand as she started to open the door of the car. "Wait a minute. There's something I did want to talk with you about before we go in. There's a man coming from England next week. His name is Harry Greenwood, and he'll be staying at Swansons' for about ten days. He has a healing ministry. Many people have been healed of serious diseases when he has prayed for them. Why don't you think about having him pray for Scott?"

"I don't know, Dan. I'll have to think about it."

Dan turned toward her, his eyes serious. "Mary, don't you think that God can heal?"

"Of course I think God can heal." Mary frowned at him. "I know God can heal. I wouldn't be sitting here right now if God hadn't healed me. Several times. I just don't know how I feel about somebody I don't even know, or who doesn't know anything about Scott, praying for healing for him."

"Mary, didn't you tell me that down in that hospital in Missouri a minister came into your room and prayed for you?"

"Yes."

"Did you know him?"

"No."

Dan hesitated. "This isn't a very kind thing to say, Mary, but I'm going to say it to you anyway. Is it possible that you don't really want God to heal Scott?"

"No, Dan. I've thought about that too. Am I subconsciously refusing to face the problem of a brain-damaged child by refusing to have him prayed for? No. That's not it."

"Well, what is it then? Why won't you let Harry pray for Scott?"

"I didn't say he couldn't, did I?" Her voice was sharp, defensive. "I said I'd have to think about it. I'm not Scott, Dan. I don't know what's right for him. I'm not God either."

"What do you mean, you're not God?"

"I mean that it's for God to decide."

"And while you're waiting for God to decide?" He left the question hanging.

"Dan. Don't push me on this. Please. I happen to feel that there are more important things than physical health."

"Oh, come on now, Mary."

"Dan, can't you see what I mean? Scott's faith in God right now is beautiful. I don't want anyone coming at him with a whole lot of 'iffings.' "

"What do you mean, 'iffings?' "

"If you do this, then God will make that happen. You know, like if we say the right combination of words, or know the right secret formula, God will heal. I just don't think that's the way God operates. What about Lazarus?"

Dan grinned at her excitement. Her cheeks were flushed. "I don't know, Mary. What about Lazarus?"

"He was dead. That's what about Lazarus."

"And so?"

"And so Jesus healed Lazarus. I mean he really healed him. Nothing Lazarus thought, felt, did, or said had anything to do with his getting up and walking out of that tomb, did it?"

Dan laughed. He opened the door of the car. "We'd better get in to the meeting; it will be half over."

As they walked down the hall the next Friday night, Scott and his mother heard the singing. Scott stopped, turned around, and looked up at Mary. "Yes?"

"What do you mean, 'yes'?"

"Didn't you put your hand on my shoulder?"

"No, I didn't touch you."

Scott looked around the empty hall, a puzzled look on his face. "But I felt someone put a hand on my shoulder."

The tall man with the English accent was praying prophetically as they entered, as if his voice were the voice of the Lord. "When you feel the touch of my hand on your shoulder, you will know that you are my child. I have chosen you."

Early the next morning, the phone interrupted the questions that Mary's mind was asking itself.

"Hi, Mary. Have you thought about it?"

"Sure I've thought about it, Dan. I've thought of nothing else."

"What have you decided?"

"Nothing." She pictured the scene in the hall at Swansons'. It had left her with a strange sense of the uncanny.

"What did Scott think of Harry? Did he say?"

"No. He was pretty sleepy when we got home. He went right to bed."

"How did you like him?"

"He's a bit flamboyant for my taste. But that doesn't necessarily mean anything."

"Why don't you put it up to Scott? If he wants to go out, I'll take him. I'll call you back."

"Never mind calling back, Dan. You win. I'll get Scott out of bed. Make it about an hour. That'll give him time to wake up."

That evening Mary stopped Scott as he walked through the kitchen, where she was peeling potatoes for supper.

"Scott, Dan told me that when you got out to Swansons' this morning, you went out on the lawn and sat on the grass for about ten minutes all by yourself. Why did you do that?"

Scott looked at his mother, his hazel eyes serious. "I wanted to pray by myself for awhile."

"What did you pray about?"

"I asked God to have Harry pray for me the way he wanted him to pray for me."

CHAPTER TWELVE

SLAVERY

Mary sat on the couch in the living room. The house was quiet. She read the journal on her lap, reviewing the past few weeks. She started at the first of October.

> I have decided I need to spend more time with Norman. If he'll only talk to me when I'm on a bar stool, I guess I have to go sit on a bar stool.

October 10
O God, I wish I were a Faulkner or a Hemingway or a Pasternak or a *somebody* who could record the pathos of the scenes I have watched since I decided to enter my husband's world, a realm the church has chosen to ignore.

How can you describe the loneliness of a bar lined with old men drinking wine? Is that all they can afford? Or is it all their stomachs can handle? Where do they take their thin faces, etched with grey veins lining stubbly cheeks, when the bartender has run his crumpled rag down the bar for the last time? What memories do they carry with them? Or have they all been flushed by the small glasses of red, filled and refilled? Do they have wives in some lonely place somewhere, wondering if they are dead— hoping, maybe? And children. Dear God, what about the children? Grandchildren, by now, no doubt. Is this the heritage you planned for them? A shake of the dice, canceled by an arm—uncontrolled little black-dotted cubes on a dirty floor?

October 16

Last night the bar was only men, shoulder to shoulder. I felt a little foolish when we walked in. I sat on the end of the bar, where it meets the wall. I asked Norm if I could have some beer nuts. I was hungry. I'm beginning to like beer. In fact, I'm a little worried. When do you stop drinking beer and it starts drinking you?

November 16

Our days are very busy. I love my nursery school job. Those children seem to approve of me totally. Quite the opposite of my husband. I can't seem to do one thing to please him anymore. I feel as if my marriage is an egg with an ever-widening crack. One of these days it is going to come oozing out, yolk and all.

Mary heard the dog barking. She closed the journal. She went into the kitchen and slipped it into the cupboard as Norm came in the door. She could tell by the smile he flashed at her that home was not his first stop after work.

"I'll have to sleep fast." He shrugged off his jacket. "I have to be back at work by two."

She looked at the clock. Her mind calculated hours and minutes. "You've been drinking for hours, haven't you?"

His eyebrows lowered. "Why the hell shouldn't I drink? All you ever do is go to church or prayer meetings. You're never home."

She clamped her lips tightly together. She walked from the room. She was sitting on the couch, reading when he walked from the kitchen toward the stairs.

"You coming to bed?" She ignored the question.

When she thought she heard his snores, she tiptoed up the stairs, into the bedroom. She sneaked her nightgown and robe from the hook on the closet door. Her husband lay on both their pillows. His mouth was open; he snored deep in his throat. She slid her hand between the two pillows, sneaking the bottom one out.

"Where in the hell do you think you're going with my pillow? Bring it back." His voice shot at her retreating back. She heard the thud as he jumped from bed. She threw the pillow behind her as she started to run. She squealed when he grabbed her hair, winced as he jerked her arm, twisting it up behind her back.

"Pick up that pillow."

She didn't move. She shut her eyes, closed her eyelids tightly together.

He pulled her arm upward, pulling hard on her hair.

"Dad, let her go, let her go."

Mary pulled away as Gretchen's voice distracted him. She ran toward the bathroom, so she could lock the door. He caught her hair and pulled her back toward the pillow, forcing her head down. She kicked the pillow hard. It hit the railing that guarded the stairs; they heard it fall with a soft "thud" as it hit the stairs.

"Dad," Gretchen's scream stopped the fist traveling toward her face. "Don't hit her, don't hit her." Gretchen scurried down the stairs. "I'll get the pillow."

Scott's hand was gentle on Mary's arm as Norm slammed the bedroom door. His hazel eyes were filled with tears. "Mother, let's go downstairs and pray."

Becca huddled on her mother's lap in the grey chair. Heidi and Gretchen sat close together on the couch. Josh sat on the floor in front of them, very still. His eyes were almost black in his white face.

Scott walked up to the bookcase. "Read a Psalm I found last week, please, Josh." He leafed through the book. "Here, the 130th."

Josh took the Bible. He closed his eyes and bowed his head. When he started reading, Mary felt the ointment of the words.

Out of the depths I cry to thee, O Lord!
Lord, hear my voice!
Let thy ears be attentive to the voice of my supplica-
tions!
If thou, O Lord, shouldst mark iniquities,
Lord, who could stand?
But there is forgiveness with thee,
that thou mayest be feared.
I wait for the Lord, my soul waits,
and in his word I hope;
my soul waits for the Lord more than watchmen for
the morning, more than watchmen for the morn-
ing.
O Israel, hope in the Lord!
For with the Lord there is steadfast love,
and with him is plenteous redemption.
And he will redeem Israel from all his iniquities.

"Let's all pray." Scott bowed his head. "Lord, O God,
we ask you to forgive us all for being so mad at Dad. O
Lord, I ask you to make this Psalm come true for him.
There is forgiveness in thee; we know that, Lord. We do
hope in your Word. We wait for your healing touch on our
father. O Lord, O God, take the fear from his heart. Help
him to trust in you. Help us, God. Help mother. God,
please don't let Dad hurt her anymore." Scott's voice
broke. Big tears sneaked out from under his eyelashes.

Josh's voice reached them softly. "God, help Dad to
know right now that we are praying because we love
him."

"Please make Dad quit drinking." Gretchen's voice was
very small. They all sat for a long quiet moment. Then
Mary spoke the words that were in her heart as tears ran
unchecked down her cheeks.

"O God, you know why I need to serve you. I don't have
to tell you. Please help Norm to see that I can't help it. You
have saved my life. You have saved my life so many times

that it isn't even my life anymore, it's yours. O Lord, please make it so this is no longer a threat to Norman. Help him, God. Help him find you. Please help him."

She put her arms around the little girl in her lap and hugged her tightly, comforted by the warmth of the small body. Heidi sat a little away from the others. Her mother did not see the cloud in her dark eyes.

After the children had gone back to bed, she wrote in her journal.

> I am going to make no bargains with Norman about God, or with God about Norman. I'm not going to say, "If you quit drinking, I'll stop going to Swansons'," or "If you quit drinking, I'll stop going to church by myself," or "I won't go unless you say that it is all right." I know a wife is supposed to be submissive to her husband. I wish I could be. I don't believe that God who loves me would expect me to be submissive to the alcohol that rules my husband's life right now. That would be to submit to the devil. When Norman is like he was tonight, he is not the man I promised to love, honor, and obey. He is some evil caricature of that man. To submit to him in this state would be to allow him to destroy me, a form of suicide. I know God does not want that. I would be no good to him completely squashed. The children need at least one parent semi-sane. The only way I can keep my sanity is to continue to accept the support of the charismatic prayer group and the church until Norm is submittable-to, if that day ever comes.
>
> So, God, you are going to have to straighten this whole mess out. I can't imagine how. Until you do, I have to go where I have people to love me and accept me and support me. I have to go where I can hear your voice. I can't hear it with my husband. Please, Lord, help me spend as much time as I can as peaceably as possible.

A week later Mary wrote again.

> This morning I was hanging up clothes, enjoying the sun on my face, the chatter of the sparrow nesting in the lilac hedge behind the clothesline when a poem started through my head. I was just about in the middle of it when the phone rang. It was Dan. He is out in Oregon at a conference on "Marriage and the Family." He said he was looking out his hotel window at the sunshine and it made him think of Scott and me, so he called to see how we are doing. Incredible how that man's mind seems to be tuned in to mine, even across a thousand miles. I don't understand it, but I thank God for it. Maybe someday I'll share this poem with Dan.

How will it be?
Like that little white cloud up there, drifting away
    from its mother?
Will it be cold—
Fragile snowflake on cherub's palm?
Or will it be warm—
Baby chicks nestling under angel hens?
Will it be loud—
Trumpet crackling thunderbolts?
Or will it be still—
Fog drifting off still waters?
Will it be dark—
Gossamer cocoon for butterfly wings?
Or will it be light—
Lightning flashing halos round the Milky Way?
Want to play opposites, God?

Mary put the book back into the cupboard, took out a cup, and poured a cup of coffee from the pot on the back of the stove. She walked up the stairs and into her bedroom where her husband was just waking up. She handed him the coffee, sat down on the side of the bed.

Scott came to the door, his eyebrows raised questioningly.

"Mother, can I talk to you a minute, later? I have something I want to tell you."

"Tell me now, Scott."

He looked at his father. "No, I'll tell you later."

"Tell me now."

Scott turned his back and walked down the hall to his room. When he came back, he held a small notebook in his hand.

"I talked to a couple of men last night after the meeting. I wrote their names down in here—here they are, Browman and Blount. I asked them to pray with me. We went into Jack's office." Scott hesitated. He looked at his father. "Mother, I told them we have a problem. I said the problem was that our father drinks too much. They prayed with me for about ten minutes. Then I lay awake, worrying that I had done the wrong thing, taking our problem to outsiders."

Mary's voice was soft and reassuring. "Scott, it's never wrong to ask anyone to pray with you about anything."

Norman put his coffee cup down on the bedside table. His eyes squinted almost shut, he asked his son, suppressed resentment leveling his voice, "Was Dan Cardiff there when you talked about me?"

"No, Dad. But these men said they were going to talk with Dan. They said he might be able to help us."

Norman didn't answer. He got out of bed. He picked up his robe. Pulling the belt tight, he walked from the room. They heard the water turn on in the shower room.

Mary wrote in her journal the next morning.

We had a lovely day yesterday. We went into Milwaukee to celebrate Scott's birthday, six months late, Scott and Norm and I. We had a grand dinner, no cocktails. Norm bought me a gorgeous red robe to save for Christmas, but I had to show it to the kids when we got home.

January 4

The caller at the railroad phoned last night about eleven. He wanted to talk with Norm. I told him he wasn't home yet. He said he had tied up at four o'clock. That meant he had been drinking at least six hours. I was so mad. I got all the liquor in the house and poured it down the sink. I arranged the beer bottles on the kitchen table, some lying on their sides. When he came in the door, I lay across the table and pretended to be drunk. He looked at me with a silly smirk and said, "Shall I go get some beer?" I was so mad I didn't sleep all night.

January 6

Norm took the job as secretary-treasurer of the union. He said he needed something to do so he wouldn't drink so much. I wonder.

January 12

Norman's drinking is much better. I'm glad he took that job. He's been working on his books at night instead of drinking. He only has two or three beers.

January 19

I sat with Scott in church instead of singing in the choir. It seems as if every time he sits still and quiet for any time at all lately, he falls asleep. I had to keep poking him to wake him up. I asked his history teacher after church if he sleeps like that in school. He said he does. I'm going to see if the doctor can give him some medicine to keep him awake.

January 26

Norman was reading in bed when the kids and I

got home from Swansons' last night. He said earlier in the day he was going with me, so I told the kids they could all go. He finked out on me. He said he had changed his mind, he had to change the points and plugs on the car. There were ten empty beer cans in the wastebasket when we got home. He had the doors all locked, and Josh had to climb in the window. Norm wouldn't answer the door. After I got into bed, he said my going to Swansons' was as bad as his going to the tavern. I didn't argue with him. I'm not going to fight about that with him. I could have told him the beauty of the worship is what allows me to live with the uncertainty of whether or not he is going to come home from work, and in what shape. I didn't try to tell him that I feel God's presence so closely when we are all singing in the Spirit or praying together. Without that, I don't think I could go on living. At least, I wouldn't want to.

January 28

Dan came over and took Scott out for a drive today. When they came back, their faces were glowing. Scott says he can pray with Dan like nobody else. Dan said he wanted to talk with me a minute. Norm was at work. He told me he was in on a prayer session with Scott and two other men out at Swansons', and that Scott had again said he thought Norm was drinking too much.

It is really none of Dan's business. I'm not going to talk about Norm's drinking with Dan. Norm revealed to me the other night that he's jealous of Dan. I think he is now reassured that there is nothing to be jealous of. I told him Dan was the only person in all the world who knew how to help us with Scott. He had to agree that this is true. I told him I have never had a more pristine relationship with any man than I have with Dan. I assured him Dan has never given me the slightest indication that he is conscious of me as a female.

All I need is to get involved with another man sexually! I feel as if I am caught in the trap of my own sexuality already. If I hadn't been so willing to settle all of our fights in bed, maybe we would have learned to communicate some other way than just with our bodies.

Scott has been showing some pretty scary symptoms. The guidance counselor called today and said that the teachers had a conference about him. They all decided we should be told that his memory is lapsing; he spends more and more time sleeping in class. Yesterday he told his dad and me that he felt dizzy in school quite often. He calls it "fuzzy vision." He said he felt yesterday as if one corner of the room were moving toward the other. Norm didn't want to talk about it. He walked away from Scott. He went to the refrigerator and took out a beer.

February 4
Dear Journal,

What would I do without you? I can't explain why, but somehow you help to straighten everything out. Norm and I had a terrible fight last night. Norm wanted me to go down and have a drink with him before the big fight started; in fact, that was what started it. I told him I wasn't going to the tavern with him any longer. I'm glad I have decided that.

He said I was "trying to force religion down his throat." I told him I had to go to Swansons' because I had to have a deeper spiritual faith to face Scott's problem. I told him he never did face it. That really made him mad. He said he faced it in his own way, "Alone." He just yelled the word at me.

I started to cry. I told him that if that was his way, it couldn't be mine, that he was being terribly cruel to me to get mad at me for looking for help. I told him I couldn't face this alone; if he wouldn't face it with me, I had to find somebody who would. I don't know what I would do without people to pray with me.

March 4
Dear Journal,

I'm sorry I haven't been writing. Nothing good to write. My head feels pretty foggy most of the time, like there was a spider in it spinning an ominous web. Scott is worse. Sleeps a lot. I think the teachers are carrying him in school just to be kind. All but his creative writing teacher. He's a mean one. I gave Scott a story I wrote. He got an A on it. He couldn't possibly stay awake long enough to write a story. I haven't talked to the doctor about his symptoms. Why? What's the use? What good would it do? Scott has had enough needles poking his arms. One real blessing is that Norm quit drinking for Lent. He started to smoke again, but who cares? Smoking can only hurt *him;* drinking smashes us all. I hope he can stay off. He has never quit for this long before, I don't think.

April 1

Really is April Fool's Day for me. I actually thought Norm quit drinking when he gave it up for Lent and then didn't start after Easter. Last night he walked in with a six-pack. I just started to cry. He said, "Why all the fuss about one six-pack of beer?"

April 12

I'm waiting for Norm to come home. I was called to school today to get Scott. He said he felt as if he were 9,500 feet above sea level, about to explode and burn up. His face was beet red. He says he is dizzy almost all the time. He says he is having more trouble with his vision, he can't see to the sides. He has a head-

ache all the time. After I brought him home, I called
Dr. Schumann. Gone. I called Dr. Levin. Gone. So I
wrote a poem.

Peel off pretense, layer by layer.
Uncover eyes, blindfolded by fear.
Look in on the malignant mass,
Its slimy tentacles of death creeping into pulsing
    brain
Until it sucks it all into itself,
Leaving empty black obscurity.
I wipe off the veneer of my faith, layer by layer.
Certitude of total surrender scribbed with the rough
    sandpaper of Truth.
Crusts of inadequacy stripped away.
Gases of fear, rebellion, self-pity, protective mother
    love
Seep through, exposing total void.
My God,
If I can put this empty shell of my faith cheek to
    cheek with
The skeletal head of death,
Can you fill them both with healing light?
Of course you can.
The question is,
Can I?

Mary was walking toward the cemetery hill, her notebook under her arm, the big golden retriever at her heels.
Her face lit up with a smile when the black convertible
pulled up beside her.

"Hi, Dan."

"Hello." Mary's face brightened at the enthusiasm in
his greeting. "Where are you going?"

She pointed to the high hill. "Up there. That's my thinking spot."

"Hop in. I'll drive you up." He reached over, opening
the door.

Mary slid into the seat, forgetting about the big dog, who ran behind the car as Dan started off.

"What were you going to your 'thinking spot' to think about, Mary?"

"A poem. I have one almost jelled in my mind. I can really write up there where the wind can blow the cobwebs away."

"I didn't know you were a poet." Dan pulled up to the highest point of the hill, pulling onto the grass. The tombstones were all behind them. The river cut a shining ribbon in the fields spreading out before them. Dan turned to Mary, asking softly, "Read me one of your poems, please, Mary?"

She leafed through the book. She didn't look at him as she read.

> Were you afraid, Mary, alone in the night?
> Did you feel terror, cold, agonized fright?
> Did you see death, so clear on the wall?
> Did you feel tears you could not let fall?
> And that last night, Mary, the night of the cross,
> The night of his death, the night of your loss,
> Did you find faith to cast out your fear,
> To hold your head high, to know God is near?

As she paused, Dan asked her, "And did Mary ever answer?"

"Yes, Dan, I think she did. One night after I came home from a meeting at Swansons' I read over what I had written. It had been a beautiful meeting. I felt really good. I wrote then—

> I was afraid, Mary, alone in the night.
> Yes, I felt terror, cold, agonized fright.
> Yes, I saw death, so clear on the wall,
> And I felt tears I could not let fall.
> But that last night, Mary, the night of the cross,
> The night of his death, the night of my loss,

God sent my son to dark Calvary.
His death gives your son Eternity.

"That's beautiful, Mary. Have you shared it with Norman?"

"No. He wouldn't want to hear it."

"How do you know? Why don't you ask him?"

Mary's eyes squinted slightly. She looked away from the man on the seat beside her.

"Mary, do you want to talk about it?"

She frowned. The big dog jumped up on the side of the car. He whined as he scratched at the door.

Mary opened the door and stepped out. She squatted down and rubbed the dog behind the ears.

"Ebbie, Ebbie boy. I forgot all about you. Did you think I was lost?"

She stood up. She closed the car door and spoke over the top to the man behind the wheel.

"I have to get home, Dan. Thanks for the ride. I'll walk back with Ebbie." Mary turned and started down the hill. Her long legs took big steps as the dog trotted beside her.

Dan ran his hand through his tight curls, shaking his head. He watched Mary and the dog go down the hill. He turned the key in the ignition, then drove slowly through the cemetery. He stopped at the stop sign, waiting for her to turn and wave as she walked away from him. The dog looked back, wagging his tail, but Mary continued on without a backward glance. He turned the car in the opposite direction. He increased his speed as he lengthened the distance between them.

CHAPTER THIRTEEN

A FAMILY ILLNESS

Mary walked out of the bedroom and closed the door. The phone in the bookcase in the hall started to ring as she walked by.

"Mrs. Soergel, this is Josh's guidance counselor. I called to tell you we have decided not to expel Josh."

"Expel him, what do you mean?"

"Do you mean to say he hasn't talked with you?"

"Talked with us about what? Why should he be expelled?"

"Josh has been skipping school, Mrs. Soergel. Didn't you know?"

"How am I supposed to know?"

"The principal called Josh into his office and talked with him about it last week. I talked with Josh yesterday. He said he had talked with you and his father, and that you told him he should handle the situation himself. Are you saying he never talked with you?"

"No. He didn't tell us a thing. How many days has he skipped?"

"Fifteen."

"Fifteen? Are you sure?"

"It may be more. Some of his excuses may be forgeries. He's been absent seventeen days in the past four weeks."

"Seventeen! Are you sure?"

"That's what our records show, Mrs. Soergel."

Mary stood by the phone after she had hung it up, her stomach knotted in a tight cramp. She hit the open palm of her left hand with her right fist in short, hard punches. The phone rang.

It was Dan's voice. "Mary, how's everything?"

"Dan. Oh, Dan. I'm so mad at Josh."

"Why?"

"He's been skipping school. His guidance counselor just called. I just hung up the phone. Josh has skipped seventeen days in four weeks. They told him he might be expelled, and he was supposed to talk with us about it. He lied. He said he did talk with us."

Dan's voice interrupted the flow of words. "Wait a minute, Mary. Wait a minute. Slow down. Things have been pretty one-sided at your house for quite a long time now. Did you ever stop to think how this might be making Josh feel?"

"No."

"You know how you feel. You have some idea of how Norm feels. What about Josh? How has all this made him feel? Think about it, Mary. Pray about it before you talk to Josh. Give him to God, Mary. He'll know what to do."

Mary walked down the stairs and into Josh's bedroom. She looked around for a clue to this son-turned-stranger. She saw the pad of paper lying beside the unmade bed, scratched-out lines and scribbling on the sheet on top. She picked it up. She squinted her eyes in an attempt to see what he had written.

> carry things inside you
> try to hide
> show your sad eyes
> while your smile lies
> what is this that cuts
> deep furrowed ruts
> in the joy that should be there
> but isn't anywhere?
> how many kinds of loneliness are there?
> My kind
> blind

what about pain?
salted rain that complains
from eyes, cries,
can you feel the shadow of an eagle passing
overhead?

Mary sat down on the crumpled bed, the paper still in her hand. She laid it down on the pillow. She picked up the stuffed dog that lay there; limp legs drooped over her fingers. One blue button stared blankly up at her. A small piece of stuffing stuck out of the hole where the other eye should have been.

"Oh, Morgan," she whispered, "what has happened to Josh? What has happened to Josh?"

The black convertible pulled up in the driveway as Mary was clearing away the breakfast dishes the next morning. She ran out of the house.

"Dan. How nice!"

"I was just driving by on my way to work. I thought I'd stop for only a minute. Is Norm home?"

"No. He was called at five this morning."

"What did he say when you told him about Josh?"

"I didn't. I was asleep when he got home." She put her hand on the door handle. "Come on in."

"Just for a minute. I have a client at 9:30."

Mary turned around to talk as she led the way. "I was so glad you called yesterday before I talked to Josh. I did just what you told me to do. I prayed about it. Do you know what happened?"

"No, Mary. What?"

"I was painting the kitchen in the afternoon. I looked at the clock at 3:20. I said to myself, 'I'm going to go find Josh.' "

"And did you find him?"

"Yes. It was really a miracle. On the way up to school I said, 'God, you are going to have to lead me to Josh. I have no idea where to start.' I drove the car the wrong way on the street that goes behind the junior high, the one marked 'Buses only.' I stopped at the stop sign and there he was. I don't know who was more surprised, me or Josh."

"What did you do then?"

"I opened the car door. I said, 'Get in, I'll take you to work.' Then I almost blew it. I said the wrong thing."

"What did you say?"

"I said, 'Well, what do you have to say for yourself?' "

"What did Josh say?"

"He just looked at me. He said, 'Nothing.' "

Dan smiled.

"Then when I told him what you had said, he kind of softened down. We talked for a long time before he went in to his job. I'm afraid Josh is a pretty mixed-up young man. I had no idea he was so terribly unhappy."

Dan's voice was soothing. "That's what happens, Mary, when a family faces a crisis such as you've been facing. Everybody is so deeply affected, they fail to see what's happening to the other members of the family. This illness of Scott's has probably been harder on Josh than on any of the other children. You said he and Scott were always very close, weren't they?"

"Yes, they were. Do you know what I thought about in the middle of the night, Dan?"

"What, Mary?"

"I thought of the time when they were real little, and we took a walk after supper. We lived in South Dakota. Scott was about four, Josh two. Scott ran on ahead. It was getting dark, so I said to Josh, 'That naughty boy. I can hardly see him, he's so far ahead of us.' Do you know what Josh said?"

"What?"

"He said, 'He is a naughty boy. How does he think we are going to find our way home?' "

Dan nodded his head. "Yes, Mary, that's just it. Josh is wondering how he's going to find his way home."

They sat quietly, and then Dan said softly, "Mary, if we could only appropriate the gifts God has given to us! Why can't we do it? Don't you dream of the day when you can go into a hospital and everybody will get up out of their beds, healed?"

Mary shook her head, "Oh, no, Dan."

He looked at her, his head to the side. "You do too, Mary."

"No. I really don't, Dan. I don't want that kind of notoriety. I don't even know how to pray for Scott. I just pray in tongues."

"In tongues! I didn't know you had the gift of tongues. Who prayed for you?"

"Nobody. One night when the Ed Soergels were here, I started all by myself in the middle of the night."

"Has it helped you, Mary?"

"Yes, Dan. I think it has. I think it has helped me handle my fear."

"That's interesting."

"I think of the gift of tongues as my personal psychiatrist. I think God has used it to show me to myself, to help me identify my own feelings. We can't do anything about a specific feeling unless we can tell what it is, can we?"

"Mary, I wish I knew what it is that God wants me to do."

"What do you mean, Dan?"

"I was lying on the couch last night, watching television. I felt completely useless. I go out and pray with Scott and he gets worse, not better. I've been haunted lately with the realization that I need to get more out into the world. Maybe God wants me to be a missionary."

"Dan, don't say that. Don't talk that way. You're a missionary right here. Think of all the people you're helping at church, and at Swansons'."

When Dan left, Mary walked up the stairs and into her bedroom. She sat down in front of her typewriter at the blue table in front of the window. She looked out at the tree that waved greening fingers at her, and began typing.

Dear Josh,

Yesterday, when the school called me, I had just gotten up off my knees where I had been praying for Scott, because I was hurting so for him. Now I think you're hurting more deeply than Scott.

It seems to me that Scott sees his role quite clearly. I think this is why he can operate with such courage. Right now, he thinks the will of God for his life is to face death with the same attitude he has faced life. He may be wrong, but he feels guided every step of the way by God. Who could ask for more? Some people never find this faith if they live to be ninety.

Your pain is more intense, your needs more complex. It seems to me, you are trying to suffer for the whole world. That's a pretty big load for a sixteen-year-old back. You don't have to carry it all by yourself. Another back has already borne it for you, and for the rest of the world. I am sure he is pleased with you. He has said, "Take up your cross and follow me." It seems to me, right now, you don't know what your cross is. I would say to you, Don't worry about it. God's timing is not our timing. I have discovered this.

He has also said to us, "Ask and ye shall receive, seek and ye shall find, knock and it shall be opened to you." You are asking; you will receive. You are seeking; you shall find. You are knocking; the door that leads to the path God wants you to travel will be opened to you. It may be a long rambling one, but you'll get there. The timing is up to God.

If I have learned anything with assurance in the past four years, it is that God answers earnest prayer. It was only after I got my own mind and my own will out of the way that God could start to answer my prayers. After I said, "Help, God! I can't do it alone, I don't think I can do it at all," he came into my life with a clear, bright light that's never gone out. Sometimes it seems to flicker, but that's my fault. It's only when my eyes are blinded by my own fear that I don't see his light. But he's a faithful God. He's a patient God. He waits until I take the blinders off, or ask him to take them off for me, and then he leads me some more.

Josh, I don't know what God's will is for you. He does. You have great potential with your sensitivity to his world, with your creative mind and seeing hands and eyes. These are gifts from God. He gave them to you. He will tell you what to do with them, not all at once, but piece by piece, glimmer by glimmer.

Turn your life over to God, day by day. You'll find the "peace that passeth understanding." Somewhere Paul talks about "joy while suffering." Our suffering is human, natural, physical. It shows. Our joy is spiritual, unseen. Perhaps the more joy we have in loving the Lord, the more we suffer as humans. I don't know. I just know I am experiencing both, intensely, simultaneously.

Yesterday Dan said to me, "Mary, turn Josh over to God." I didn't tell him that every night since you were born, I have asked God to guide your steps.

Love,
Mother

One day's journal entry read:

The family is scattering for the summer. Scott got back the result of his college preps. He's still in the upper seven percent of his class in the nation. Norm said that proves he's healthy enough to go to work in the conservation camp. Dr. Crawford wrote, urging us to send him back to Boston for evaluation. I thought he should go to Boston. Norm and Scott thought he should go to camp. They won.

I think this time Norm means it about quitting the booze. I haven't seen any evidence lately that he's been drinking. He's been coming home when he ties up.

She heard the car in the driveway. She put the journal in the cubbyhole and waited to greet her husband. Her lips clamped together when she saw what he held in his hand as he came in the door from the garage. She leaned back against the counter. Her legs suddenly felt weak. She put her clenched fist on her mouth, as if to hold in the anger she felt rising until it reached her tongue with the taste of rotten copper.

Norm put the narrow brown sack he carried on the table. He separated the beer can from its plastic ring, pulled off the tab top. He reached in the brown paper bag and pulled out a bottle. Mary watched him walk to the cupboard and take out a juice glass. He poured it full of the amber liquid. Meeting her eyes defiantly, he raised it to his lips. It was empty when he put it down on the table.

She swallowed and sat down.

"Norm, I want to talk to you about something. I've been having second thoughts about taking Scott up to camp. Dr. Crawford said he thought he should go to Boston. I think we should go up to camp and see Scott next Sunday."

"No."

"Why not?"

"The tires on the car aren't good enough. They might not make the trip."

"How come they were good enough to get him up there then?"

"Damn it! I said *no!*" He hit his fist against the table.

Mary ran from the kitchen. She lay down on her bed, pulling the pillow over her head. The phone rang. As it rang on, she realized Norm wasn't going to answer. She sat up on the bed, blowing her nose hard.

"Mary, are you all right?" It was Dan's voice.

"Oh hi, Dan. I'm fine, I just have a little cold." She sniffed into the phone.

"I called to see if you have an address for Scott. I have a little free time; I thought I'd drop him a line."

Mary stood in the front yard. The words they had thrown at each other were so vicious that she felt she had to get out of the house after her husband had left for work, as if to escape the fumes that lingered in the air from their anger. She walked into the garage and looked at the wall where her husband had hung his tools. She picked up the hatchet. She walked back to the big stump in front of the picture window in the kitchen. She raised the hatchet high in the air, swung it hard against the top of the stump. She sat down on top of the stump, wood chips flying around her as she bent her elbow in rapidly repeated swings.

"Mary, who are you trying to kill?"

Mary looked at the man who spoke to her from the low black convertible in front of the house.

"Dan, where did you come from?"

"I passed a strawberry stand and thought you might be able to use some." He held out a quart box of bright red berries.

"Why, thanks, Dan." Mary looked toward the house. She saw Heidi looking out the kitchen window at them. "I'll be right out. I'll take these in and tell the kids we're going to go for a ride, all right?"

He looked at her. Uncertainty washed over his face.

"I don't want to talk here, Dan. I'm too upset."

A few minutes later, Dan looked over at Mary, then fixed his eyes on the road as he drove toward the little lake north of the subdivision.

"Why are you upset, Mary?"

"Oh, Norm and I had a little disagreement. I wanted to

go see Scott. He said the tires on the car aren't good enough."

Dan turned onto the narrow gravel road that led to the lakeshore. He pulled the car up by the lake and shut off the motor. The breeze that ruffled the water stirred up the tight curls in his hair. They danced gaily, a contrast to his sober expression.

"Mary, I asked you about this once before. You wouldn't talk about it. I think you need to talk about it. Is Norm drinking too much?"

Mary bit her lower lip. Tears rimmed the edges of her eyelashes. Her throat tightened. The words couldn't escape. She felt as if even her breath couldn't get through the constriction. She shook her head from side to side.

"Mary." Dan's voice took on an edge, cutting at her. "If this is a problem, you need help with it. You can't handle it alone. Tell me. Is Norman drinking too much? You have to face it, Mary. You have to face it."

Silence dropped a shroud between them. Mary sat with bent head. Tears polkadotted her slacks.

When he realized she wasn't going to answer him, Dan started the motor. They drove back to her house without speaking.

Mary looked across the seat at him when he stopped the car. He saw the hazel eyes clouded with pain. "I'm sorry, Dan. I'm sorry," she whispered softly.

Mary left a note on the kitchen table. "I have gone grocery shopping. Back in about an hour."

She saw the black convertible parked outside the church as she drove by. She pulled over, walked up the steps and through the wide white doors. Charlie was sitting with Dan on the steps leading up into the sanctuary. Dan got up when he saw Mary.

"Mary, I was just wishing I could talk with you. Do you have a moment?"

Mary felt suddenly uneasy. Dan's voice sounded so impersonal; the usual warmth was missing. He avoided her eyes. Mary looked at Charlie. He shrugged his shoulders. She could not read the expression in his eyes.

"Sure, Dan."

"Come on. Let's go up into the lounge." Dan turned as he started up the aisle. "Thanks for listening, Charlie."

Charlie nodded at Dan's retreating back. He patted Mary's arm. As she followed Dan's back down the green carpeted aisle, between the pews in this room where she had first joined the church, been married, held babies to be baptized, Mary wondered at the expression in the minister's eyes. Why had Charlie looked at her like that?

Mary sat down on a chair just inside the door, looking at Dan with a puzzled expression. He was standing looking out the window, his back toward her. When he swiveled around, his eyes darted to her face, then looked quickly away. He spoke to the wall above her head.

"I don't know quite how to tell you this, Mary, but God has been telling me that you belong over here," he pointed to one side of the room, "and I belong over there." His finger moved towards the farthest corner.

Mary's eyes followed the pointing finger, as if it might be directing her to an answer to the startled question mark that had stamped itself on her brain as he spoke.

"I've been thinking about your marriage, Mary, and about your children. I've been thinking about Norm. I've thought a lot about Norman, Mary." He hesitated. His eyes flicked away from her face.

"I'm going to take a new job that has opened up in Oregon."

Mary's eyes widened. She felt as if she had breath enough for only two words. "You're leaving?"

"Yes. Next week. I've been offered a tremendous opportunity. Do you remember the conference I attended last spring on 'Marriage and the Family?' I met a man at that time who is chairman of the board for a foundation that is setting up a new clinic to treat the family as a complete entity, a new concept in counseling. He has asked me to become the first director. He has offered me unlimited freedom. I feel very honored."

He went on, as if unaware of how she was feeling.

"I was just talking to Charlie about it when you came in." His tone took on vibrancy, his eyes shone as he continued. "It's a very exciting prospect, Mary, a challenge and a new adventure. I will be working with the ministers' council in Portland. I plan to start weekly prayer meetings. You know how many times I have told you that I think the charismatic movement belongs in the orthodox churches in order to avoid the splintering off that occurred during the Pentecostal revival the first part of this century. Just think, Mary, God has offered me an opportunity to be a disciple."

He began pacing up and down in front of the windows. "Mary," vibrancy changed to urgency in his tone as well as his words, "if the charismatic movement doesn't wedge itself into the historic churches, it is going to die. It's inevitable. Man's ego is too strong, his urge for power too great to forego the discipline and restraint of the churches. We cannot turn our backs on the length and depth of the past as we reach towards the height of our present. Where has the Holy Spirit done his work down through the ages? God has used the churches, in spite of fumblings and weaknesses, their obsession with their own ideas, their lack of vision, their obtuse blindness to what God is trying to show them. God is giving us another chance, Mary. The charismatic movement could grow from a trickle to a wave big enough to open the Red Sea once more, to lead God's children away from the horror that is gaining ground, if we will only open our eyes and look into the future."

Dan paused a moment, looking down at Mary. She saw a flicker of the old concern in his eyes. "I've prayed much about this, Mary. It is not an impulsive move. I've been in a real agony of indecision. Then, the other day I was in a bookstore and I found this little book which confirms all my ideas about the need for the churches to be open to the moving of the Holy Spirit. The first three chapters are written by my favorite contemporary prophet, Michael Ramsey. Here, take it, I want you to have it." He dropped the red paperback on her lap. Mary picked it up. She looked at the large white words, *The Charismatic Christ*, as Dan went on.

"I have to go to Portland, Mary. I feel the wind of the Spirit like a tornado on my back."

He waited for her reply. Her breath felt shallow in her chest.

Dan's eyes lost their light when she looked up at him, wordlessly. Only her eyes spoke to him. They looked large in her white face. The hazel was hidden by dark grey clouds, filled with tears.

Almost inaudibly he breathed the words that were to come back to taunt her. "You know, in a way it will be a real relief."

He turned and walked from the room.

Mary spent the rest of the day escaping her feelings by groping for the words that blew around in her mind. When the children were in bed, she reached for her journal, tucked her legs beneath her, chewed on the eraser of her pencil, then started to scribble rapidly on the lined pages.

> Shattered, broken, splintered, fractured,
> The trinkets all fell from my Christmas tree.
> Lights flicker out, erasing love's imagery.
> Hope betrayed by a life thought safe.
> Stars pulled from eyes,
> As blinders slide through fingers salty wet.
> My hands relinquish crumbling shell of trust's
>   facade.
> Empty hands.
> Why, Lord?
> To find a little more hay for the manger?

A wine bottle to fetch for your filling?
Knead bread for a shared loaf?
But who's to share?
But who's to share?
Do I hear the angels sing?
Do prophetic voices ring?
"Christ only worthy,
Christ only free,
Christ alone, sufficiency."
My lesson of Gethsemane, taught by a broken
    Christmas tree?

Dan stood in front of the fireplace in Jack's office. The usual smile lines around his eyes were erased. His face was white and drawn. When he spoke, his eyes looked as if they had lowered the shades and closed up shop; there was nothing on display. His tone was level, tightly controlled as he said, "I think God wants me to leave here."

Karen sounded shocked. "Leave? What do you mean, Dan? You think that God wants you to move?"

"Yes, that's exactly what I mean. I have been offered a job in Oregon, as director of a newly established clinic to deal with family relationships, working directly with the clergy in the city. I would have a chance to implement solutions for some of the problems I am unable to deal with at present."

"Like what, Dan?" Jack sounded interested.

"Marriage, for one. I think it is about time the churches returned to the concept of marriage as God intends it, as he spells out specifically in his Word over and over—one woman married to one man, forever. I am so nauseated by the phrase 'meaningful relationship,' I feel like hitting the next mouth that says it to me. Day after day I hear people talk about 'meaningful relationships' as an excuse to break up a marriage. A year later, I see the same people, looking for another 'meaningful relationship.' They're chasing a mirage through a mist of their own making."

As Dan spoke, Karen's mind asked the question that had so often puzzled her. "Is that why he has never married?"

She was startled as Dan looked at her with a perception that seemed to have read her thoughts. His eyes shot out a dart of hostility, resenting the intrusion of her diagnostic musing. He looked at Jack as he continued.

"The real tragedy is that alcoholism is involved in many of these fractured relationships, the unrecognized villain of the play. This is what I intend to urge the clergy to understand, the role they play in supporting the disease alcoholism, or drug addiction."

Jack's forehead creased in a puzzled frown. "What do you mean, Dan? How do ministers support alcoholism?"

Interest in what they were discussing pulled up the shades. Dan's blue eyes heated, the sparks shot into his voice, vibrating it.

"Yesterday I had a couple come into my office. Their oldest son had been killed recently in a motorcycle accident. He had been drinking with his gang, probably using drugs as well. It doesn't matter now. He's dead. It took one hour's interview for me to realize the mother is alcoholic. She had been counseling with her minister for four years. Four years! And now her son is dead."

Karen's voice was shocked. "Dan, you're not saying that the son's death was the minister's fault?"

Dan's tone was hard, decisive.

"Karen, in my vocabulary there is no such word as 'fault' or 'blame' or 'bad' or 'wrong' when dealing with alcoholism. Alcoholism is a disease. A minister has no more right to try to treat alcoholism than he has to treat cancer."

"But did he know the woman was alcoholic?"

"That's just the point. That's what I want to do on this new job, help the clergy recognize the disease, instead of trying to treat an illness until the patient and his family get sick and die. No minister is equipped to recognize the lies and deceit that make up the alcoholic behavior pattern without special training. I aim to see that they get that training."

"But, Dan, we need you. I think you need a fellowship, Dan. I can't bear to think of you going off all alone."

"I know, Karen. That's why I've been so tormented. I need you too. This fellowship has been the family I never had, the relationships I could never establish until we were all filled with the Spirit and came to love and trust one another. But that has been part of the message God has seemed to be giving me. He has been showing me that I have to move beyond depending on human relationships to a deeper dependence on him. It seems to me, Karen, that there is a danger even in loving and trusting. These very blessings could become a barrier between us and the will of God if we allow them to be."

Karen's voice sounded hurt as she asked, "What do you mean, Dan?"

"It would be easy to make an idol of human relationships. We could avoid the pain of parting from one another, and deny the will of God for our lives. That is what I think I would be doing if I didn't take this new job."

"But, Dan, what about Scott? How is he going to get along without you?"

Dan stood up straighter. He looked directly into Karen's eyes as he spoke. She saw the pinpricks of pain in his eyes, the sharp points of agony that tore his voice, raveling the edges.

"Karen, as I listened to that family yesterday, I saw myself. I realized that I have been playing the same role in Mary's life as the minister who failed to recognize the disease alcoholism, only for me there is no excuse. I know the symptoms. I recognized them long ago."

Karen's shocked voice interrupted him. "Dan, Mary's no alcoholic."

"I know, Karen, but Norm is. My support of Mary is allowing Norm to avoid facing his responsibilities. I am allowing him to continue to drink by playing the roles he should be playing."

Jack spoke from across the desk. "What roles do you mean, Dan?"

"Mary talks with me about the things she should discuss with Norm. Scott turns to me when he should turn to his father."

"But Norm won't talk to Mary, Dan. She's shared that with me, how important your listening has been to her."

"Exactly. I am trained to listen. I am a psychologist. Norm can't listen. He's sick. He never will be able to listen until he is forced to face his illness, until Mary is forced to face it. She is denying it. I have tried to talk with her about it several times, but she refuses to discuss it."

"But, Dan, Mary knows Norm drinks too much. She has talked about it with me. Maybe she feels it would be disloyal to Norm to discuss it with you."

"Karen, that's why I am trying to explain. Alcoholism is a disease. It would be no more disloyal for Mary to discuss it with me than if Norm had diabetes. The alcoholic is a guilt-wracked, suffering, terrified human being who realizes he needs help but is afraid to ask for it, because to ask for help would mean giving up what he worships as God in his life, the liquor he thinks he needs to go on living. The wife of an alcoholic becomes sick also, trying to cope with all the destruction this disease engenders. Mary is sick right now, Karen, even if you can't see it. She needs help too, but I can't give it to her. The best help I can give is to get out of her life completely."

"But, Dan..."

Jack interrupted the flow of her words. "Karen, Dan knows what he is doing. He said he thinks this is what God wants him to do. We have to accept that."

"Thanks, Jack." Dan put his arm around Karen's shoulders as she stood up, squeezing her hard. His eyes filled with tears as he took the hand Jack offered him. They walked from the room in silence.

The wheels of the convertible spit gravel. Jack put his arm around his wife as they stood at the door of the porch watching Dan drive down the long curving drive, past the lake, over the bridge, and out of sight.

Karen sighed. She wondered how Mary was feeling. If she could have read what Mary was writing, she would have known.

Mary was scrunched up in her bed, her notebook on her knees. The light on the table by her bed was the only light in the house as she wrote.

> I looked at death and cried.
> I was afraid.
> I stood alone.
> You took my hand.
> You said, "Come, we will look at death together."
> We stood still on the plain,
>   in transcedent community with God and with
>   eternity.
> You looked back at life.
> You dropped my hand.
> I looked at death and cried.
> I was afraid.
> I stood alone.

A sound in the hall drew her eyes off the notebook.

"Why, Scott, I thought you were asleep."

Scott sat down on the bed beside her, putting the Bible he carried in his lap. His hand felt warm on her arm. His eyes were luminous.

"Mother, I have to tell you something." Scott's voice was intense. His hands cut the air with sharp quick thrusts, as if to break through an invisible barrier.

"Mother, I'm not afraid to die. How can we help Dad realize that? One time in the hospital, I don't remember what hospital, what operation, Jesus said to me, 'Don't be afraid, Scott. I am with you. I will be with you forever. I am with you in this hospital. I will be with you in eternity.' "

Scott narrowed his eyes in reflection. He ignored the tears running down his mother's face. "I felt him, Mother. I could almost touch him, I knew so surely that Jesus was right there." He shook his head in wonder. "How could I be afraid, Mother, after I have felt the presence of God?"

Mary shook her head, wiping her cheeks with her hand.

"How can we help Dad? How can we help him accept this?"

Mary shrugged her shoulders helplessly.

Scott picked up the Bible that lay in his lap. "I was just reading John 14, Mother. I had to come and share it with you. Here, Jesus says to his disciples, 'If you love me, obey me; and I will ask the Father and he will give you another Comforter, and he will never leave you. He is the Holy Spirit, the Spirit who leads into all truth. The world at large cannot receive him, for it isn't looking for him and doesn't recognize him. But you do, for he lives with you now and some day shall be in you. No, I will not abandon you or leave you as orphans in the storm—I will come to you.' "

Scott paused, his finger on the page. "That's what he did, Mom. He came to me." He continued, his voice almost a whisper.

" 'In just a little while I will be gone from the world, but I will still be present with you. For I will live again—and you will too. When I come back to life again, you will know that I am in my Father, and you in me, and I in you. The one who obeys me is the one who loves me; and because he loves me, my Father will love him; and I will too, and I will reveal myself to him.'

"Oh, Mother. It seems so simple to me. I wish Dad could see it too. If Jesus is in me, and I am in Jesus, it doesn't make any difference where I am, here or in heaven. Jesus is in you too, through his Holy Spirit, so I will be with you, whether I am alive or whether I have died. Isn't that right, Mother?"

Mary could only nod.

"Do you know what my very favorite part of the Bible is, Mother? I read it almost every day. It is really a comfort to me. Do you want me to read it to you?"

Mary nodded again. As he leafed through the green *Living Bible*, Mary noticed the signs of wear, the dog-eared pages, underlined words, and loose binding. When Scott began reading, his voice was softly affectionate, as if the words were old and very dear friends.

" 'No, for the Scriptures tell us that for his sake we must be ready to face death at every moment of the day—we are like sheep awaiting slaughter, but despite all this, overwhelming victory is ours through Christ who loved us enough to die for us. For I am convinced that nothing can ever separate us from his love. Death can't, and life can't. The angels won't, and all the powers of hell itself cannot keep God's love away. Our fears for today, our worries about tomorrow, or where we are—high above the sky, or in the deepest ocean—nothing will ever be able to separate us from the love of God demonstrated by our Lord Jesus Christ when he died for us.' "

Scott closed the Bible. He put his hand over his mother's hand. She felt his warm fingers squeeze hers as Scott said, "Let's pray for Dad, shall we, Mother?"

CHAPTER FOURTEEN

A DYING MARRIAGE

"What did you think, Norm, when Josh got off the train?"

He smiled across the kitchen table at his wife. "Who's that character?"

"That's the way I felt. I wonder if the men working on the train knew that was your son with the long hair and bare feet."

"That hair!" Norm wrinkled his nose. He dipped his knife in the peanut butter jar. "That's the first thing we're going to change."

Mary thought about how hard Josh had worked so he could visit friends in California. He had returned home a different person. Had he changed only in appearance?

Her thoughts switched to Scott. "Norm," Mary paused, groping for the right words. "I've been thinking. Scott's still sleeping an awful lot. Maybe we had better take him to see Dr. Levin."

"Send him back to Boston. Those guys really know what they're doing."

"But, Norm, what if his sleeping means the tumor is recurring. Boston is pretty far..."

"Mary," the sharp voice interrupted her. "I don't want to know the latest thing you've imagined. You think too much. Take him to see Ben Schumann. Start with him. We'll see what he says. Then we'll talk." He got up from the chair. "I have to go to work. Any socks in my drawer?"

Mary stood by the kitchen counter two days later, packing the lunches for school, when Scott came in the room.

"What did Dad say, Mother?"

"I didn't get a chance to ask him, Scott. He didn't get home until after two, and he was in no shape to talk."

"Call Dr. Crawford then, please, Mom."

"Scott, I think I'd better wait until your father gets up and talk it over with him."

"Wait for Dad! What good does that ever do? He insisted I see Dr. Schumann. He did a blood test. A blood test, what good did that do?" Scott's voice rose to a shout. He pounded his fist on the counter. A spoon rattled off onto the floor. "I'm sick of this, I'm sick of it, I'm sick of it."

Mary looked at her son's red face. Her voice was quiet as she said, "You're right, Scott. I'll call Dr. Crawford."

"Oh, hi, Norm. I didn't hear you drive in. Eb must be with the kids."

Mary put down the pile of plates she had been stacking on the picnic table in the backyard as her husband walked toward her. He lifted her off the ground with a hard squeeze, kissing her quickly.

"Where are the kids?" Norm picked up the bottle of ketchup as they walked into the house.

"Out there somewhere." She waved at the fields that rimmed the cluster of houses. "Down at the river, maybe. They said something about seeing a lot of carp while we were eating. Did you eat?"

"I had a snack on the way home. Scott with the other kids?"

"No. He's upstairs sleeping."

Norm walked over to the refrigerator as Mary squirted soap in the sink she was filling with hot water.

"What did the doctor say?"

"He didn't tell Scott a thing."

Norm turned toward her, his voice sharp. "What do you

mean, he didn't tell Scott anything? Why didn't you talk to him?"

Mary turned from the sink. She wiped her soapy hands on her apron. "Why? Scott's the one who knows how he feels." She leaned back against the sink, her eyes narrowing just a little. "Scott was so upset that I called Dr. Crawford. He said he thought it was a good idea to see Dr. Levin first and then, if the situation warrants it, we could send him to Boston. So I called Dr. Levin. He wasn't in. They're going to have him call me back tomorrow."

Norm took two steps toward his wife. He pointed his finger, his eyes blazing as he shouted, "You shouldn't have called Dr. Levin without asking me first. It's about time you found out that there are two parents in this family."

Mary shut her lips tightly together. She marched out to the picnic table, her back ramrod stiff. She walked back into the kitchen and plunked down a tray on the table.

"You talk to Dr. Schumann then."

"I will. Tomorrow."

"What am I going to say to Dr. Levin when he calls?"

The fist pounded the table. "I don't care what you tell him. It was your idea to call him, not mine. It's about time you quit playing doctor around here." The finger pointed accusingly. "You always think you know it all. The only reason Scott isn't in school is because you think he can't go. You're trying to make an invalid out of him."

Mary ran from the kitchen. She took the steps two at a time as she ran up the stairs. She threw her clothes at the bed as she took them off, and grabbed her husband's terry cloth robe from the hook on the back of the bedroom door. She ran for the shower room down the hall, but suddenly turned. She ran back down the stairs and outside. Norm was sitting at the picnic table, beer can in hand, the paper open before him.

Her hands were on her hips. The words spouted from her mouth, a fountain of anger. "Norman Soergel, I would

like to remind you that I took your son to see Dr. Schumann the day he fell down the stairs. Dr. Schumann said
there was nothing wrong. That night he fell down the
stairs in a convulsion. Was that my imagination? Did I
imagine the brain tumor so I could have an invalid for a
son?"

She stood taller. She pulled the ends of the belt, and the
terry cloth around her waist bunched in resistance. Her
voice rising, she said, "When he was so fat, was that my
imagination? Then why did Dr. Crawford put him in the
hospital? What about the conservation camp—is that why
I let you talk me into letting him go, to make an invalid out
of him?"

Her clenched fists hit the picnic table as she leaned over
and glared into her husband's eyes. "Do you know what's
the matter with you? You're a coward. You can't face it.
You're afraid to face the truth. If Scott can face it, the least
we can do is face it with him."

Norman stood up, crouching forward with his mouth
twisting in his reddening face. He raised his fist and
shook it in Mary's face. "Go get some clothes on. You look
like some kind of slut."

Mary came down the back steps carrying a black loose-
leaf notebook. Her voice was ice cold. "May I have a
check, please?"

"What do you want a check for?"

"Groceries."

"I'll take you to your Diaconate meeting. Then I'll do the
shopping. You can't drive the car in your condition."

Mary wheeled around. She walked into the garage and
threw the notebook into her bike basket. As she neared
the crest of the hill, the sobs that she had tried to push
back came shuddering out. The notebook fell from the
basket as the bike swayed. As her legs pushed against the
resistance of the steep incline, her tight skirt rose well

above her knees. She snatched at it as the boys in the car that passed her pointed, laughing.

"Who is it?" Her mother's voice called out from the bedroom as she walked in the front door of her parents' home.

"It's me. I'm supposed to be at a Diaconate meeting, but I can't go." She sat down opposite her father in the living room, putting her hands over her face. "I'm sorry I'm crying, but I'm so mad."

"What's the matter?" Her father looked at her from over the top of his glasses.

She blew her nose. "Oh, Norm's mad at me because I called to make an appointment for Scott to see Dr. Levin."

Her mother's bedroom slippers shuffled toward her. There was a puzzled look in the blue eyes. "Why should that make him mad?"

"He doesn't like Dr. Levin. He's never liked him since he said Scott was going to die."

Her mother looked down at her. "Can you stay here tonight?"

"I'd like to."

Her father's brows lowered as he looked at his wife. "Maybe she should go home."

"No. She's going to stay here. You call Norman. I'll get you a sleeping pill, Mary. You'll feel better if you have a good night's sleep."

Mary got up the next morning and drank a quick cup of coffee. She then sat down at her father's typewriter and wrote a long letter to Dr. Levin, detailing Scott's recent symptoms. As she was finishing the letter, Norman walked in the back door.

"Come on. I've come to take you home."

"I'm writing to Dr. Levin. I want to finish first."

He turned and without a word walked out of the house. Mary heard the car leave the driveway as her father came out of his bedroom.

"Didn't I hear Norm's voice? Where did he go?"

She was tired of hiding the truth from her parents. "Down to the tavern, probably."

"Oh, no, he couldn't be doing that. It's only nine o'clock in the morning."

Mary's twisted smile was the only answer. She felt defeated.

When her father took her home three hours later, her husband's car was not in the garage. Neither one of them commented on that fact. Mary opened the door, jumping from the car.

"Bye, Dad. Thanks for the ride."

She ran in the house. Becca ran up to her. She threw her arms around her mother's legs. She began to cry, a soft whimper. Mary felt the moist warmth against her legs. She picked up her child and sat down in the large grey chair. She buried her head in her daughter's hair.

CHAPTER FIFTEEN

RELAPSE

"Norm." Mary spoke to her husband as he walked in the kitchen door. "Dr. Levin called today. He wants Scott to go into St. Luke's for testing. He said he would call me back when he gets a bed for him."

Norman looked at his wife, his eyes narrowing. He walked into the next room. Mary followed, waiting as he took off his jacket and hung it over the back of a dining room chair. She was unable to read anything from the tone of his voice. "Where are all the kids?"

"I just sent Gretch out to call them for supper. It's all ready."

"Good. I was thinking on the way home that it's about time we got organized around here. I'm going to have a talk with those jokers."

Supper was strangely subdued. After they had eaten in almost total silence, Norm pushed back his chair. He reached into his shirt pocket, pulling out a piece of paper.

"I have something to say to all of you. I'm sick and tired of living in a pigpen. I'm tired of being the only one who does any work around here. I want these jobs done before I come home tomorrow. Josh, you can clean the garage and clean the basement. I want you to put all those bottles that have been cluttering up the back porch in paper bags and put them in the trunk of the car tonight. It doesn't make much sense to have all that money tied up in pop bottles, now, does it?"

Mary bit back the automatic response as she calculated

the amount invested in six pop bottles as opposed to six cans of beer. She felt her neck tighten in resentment as she heard him continue.

"Heidi and Gretchen, you can scrub the kitchen floor and defrost that filthy refrigerator. I don't know who you think pays the electric bills around here. That's another thing; nobody ever turns off a light except me. Every time I come home I see every light in this house blazing, like you were trying to light up the whole town."

"I told you we need a new light cord, Dad. You said you would fix it last month. We can't reach it unless we stand on a chair." Little Heidi's temper was as fiery as her father's. Her brown eyes blazed in reflection of his.

"If you kids would take care of things, I wouldn't always have to be fixing things around here. I feel like the whole place is falling apart. Damn it, it's about time I got some cooperation around here!"

Josh jumped off his chair as a blue car, a red flame painted on the door, squealed into the drive, scattering gravel.

"Sorry, Dad. I have to go." He ran from the room and down the front walk. His long hair waved a defiant farewell.

The girls pushed back their chairs.

"Sit down! I'm not through with you."

"I have to do my homework, Dad." Gretchen's round face had a determined expression. "I have a science project that's due tomorrow."

"And who's going to do the dishes? I'm tired of dirty dishes sitting in the sink until somebody gets a little ambition."

"I'll do them," Heidi called back as she walked toward the stairs, "but not until you get out of the kitchen."

Mary looked at Scott. He sat with his elbows resting on the table. He held his head between his hands.

"I'll go talk to them, Norm."

Gretchen was lying on her bed. She didn't give her

mother a chance to begin. "Listen to me, mother. All he does is yell and swear at us. He would never, never, never listen to us when we want to talk to him about anything. Then he comes at us with his lists and starts ordering us around like we're the convicts and he's the warden."

Heidi's voice accused her mother from where she lay on the bed beside her sister. "Nobody ever listened to me anyway, since Becca was born." Mary turned and walked out of the room.

Three nights later she wrote in her journal.

> We saw Dr. Levin yesterday. Scott slept soundly all the time we were waiting to get in to see him. I sat and prayed for fresh guidance for the doctor, for help for me and Norm to face this thing together. Please, God. When we got home, I felt like I just had to get out of the house by myself. I walked up the cemetery hill and walked around between the gravestones. I felt like David must have when he wrote, "O Lord, what is man, that thou art mindful of him?" The wind was blowing very hard, there were storm clouds flying close above me. I raised my hands in the air. I cried out to God. I felt very alive, very stirred with despair as the lightning flashed, a white-hot knife in my gut. It seems as if I'm in a nightmare I've dreamed before. Why can't I have enough faith not to react like this each time?
>
> I don't know why we bothered to see the doctor. He was very noncommittal. He said he thinks Scott should go in the hospital. Norm won't talk about it. God, what are we going to do? Please help us.
>
> Tuesday
> I'm in the lobby of St. Luke's. Scott is having EEG, brain scan. We stopped for a hamburger on the way in. I felt so insulated from the people in there at the tables near us. Next to us there were two mothers with their little boys, talking about playing golf and

the party at the country club. They were so absorbed with it. I wondered if this is the way blacks feel about whites—so separated from their pleasant world.

It's almost harder each time. It is harder. It's as if all the feelings you have had all the other times come back to pile up on you. God, I feel squashed.

Saturday

The promise to start a prayer group that I made at the Spiritual Life Retreat led by Nate Thorpe has been bugging me for months, but I was afraid another prayer meeting would be one more threat to Norm. So I put it off, until Charlie reminded me of it. I told him OK, but it would have to be at seven o'clock Saturday morning. I figured Norm would probably be sleeping one off at that hour. I was right. We had our first meeting this morning. Only six people showed up.

I saw Dr. Levin, finally. He said he is pretty sure the tumor has recurred. He wants to put Scott in surgery and do a pneumoencephalogram and an arteriogram on Monday. That's really the only way they can be sure. It's actually seeing what the circulation in the head is doing, and being able to X-ray the head with the air in it, that will tell if there is foreign matter to be removed.

Sunday night

Josh, Becca, and I went in to spend the afternoon with Scott. He said he had been so dizzy in church that he had to leave. About three o'clock he said, "Do you kids mind if Mom prays for me? Let's go down to the chapel." We sat in silence for a long time and then Josh said, "Dear Lord, thank you for sending us our troubles; they teach us we really need you."

Mary was awakened the next morning by the sound of

the phone outside the bedroom door. She pulled on her robe, then walked out into the hall and picked up the receiver.

"Mrs. Soergel, this is Dr. Levin."

Mary interrupted the doctor's voice. "Just a minute, Dr. Levin. I want to put my husband on this phone. I'll go downstairs."

"My associates and I have concluded," the doctor continued when she picked up the downstairs phone, "that although there is no sign of tumor, the problems Scott has been having are caused by pressure. The pressure is caused by the cerebrospinal fluid which is accumulating in the spaces formerly occupied by the tumor. The fluid pooling in the cavities is causing the same symptoms the tumor originally caused. The body produces about a pint of cerebrospinal fluid daily. In the normal person, the fluid circulates freely between the ventricles of the brain. Then it's absorbed into the bloodstream."

Mary heard her husband's breathing on the upstairs phone as the doctor went on. "In Scott's head, because of the amount of pressure from the tumor before it was removed, the brain was pushed up tightly against the skull, so that the blood vessels were unable to carry away the fluid. This is happening again. We feel Scott needs a shunt. This is a tube which we put into the head, between the ventricles. We insert it in the carotid artery in the neck. The shunt would lead from the brain down through the carotid directly to the heart. The heart will take care of the fluid that's pooling in the brain at present."

"When would you operate?" Mary asked.

"Monday."

"What do you think, Norm?"

"I'm thinking."

The doctor talked rapidly. "You talk it over. I'll be out of town over the weekend. Please let the floor nurse know your decision so we can schedule the surgery."

"I feel better." Mary put the coffeepot on the back

burner. She spoke to her husband as he walked into the kitchen. "At least that explains why Scott has been so sleepy all the time."

"Call Dr. Crawford. See what he says."

"Right now?"

"Right now."

Dr. Crawford's slow voice gave Mary instant confidence. "I would ask Dr. Levin to consult with Dr. Sweet. That's your prerogative. It's always a good idea to call for a consultation when two doctors have been involved."

Mary dialed the phone. The voice at the other end was crisp.

"I'm sorry. Dr. Levin is out of town until Monday. I have no number where he can be reached. Would you like to speak with Dr. Evekewicz?"

Mary replied in the negative. She took a cup from the cupboard and poured from the pot on the back of the stove. She sat down opposite her husband at the kitchen table. "What do we do now?"

"Get Scott out of that damn hospital. I think we should send him to Boston. If Dr. Crawford and Dr. Sweet think he needs a shunt, they can do it in Boston."

"But Dr. Levin isn't going to be back until Monday."

"So? We don't need him. We'll just go in and take him out."

The next night she wrote in her journal.

> Josh and I are supposed to go to a retreat tomorrow at Green Lake. Norm said to go ahead and go, that he would lay off and stay home with the kids. I feel uneasy leaving Scott. I have had a week of deep soul-searching after we found out there was no tumor. I have considered my lack of faith. I remembered all the times Dan wanted me to have Scott prayed for and I refused.
>
> How great is our God. He doesn't need me. No matter how I feel, no matter how I fear, he doesn't let

happen what I am afraid of happening. He prevents it from happening. He doesn't depend on my feeling. Praise the Lord.

Last night a miracle took place in our living room. Norman led a prayer service. After supper he said to all of us, "Come into the living room." There, with no explanation, he began to read Psalm 23. He has a very melodious voice. Those words have never sounded more lovely to me. "The Lord is my shepherd, I shall not want." Next he read Psalm 27. "The Lord is my light and my salvation; whom shall I fear? The Lord is the stronghold of my life; of whom shall I be afraid?" Then the miracle compounded itself. He read Psalm 40. I have never shared with him what happened the night I found out about Scott's brain tumor, when I opened the Bible to Psalm 40, which has been my guide ever since. What a feeling to have Norm read, in that same living room, the Psalm God used to comfort me.

When Norm spoke the words, "He drew me up from the desolate pit, out of the miry bog, and set my feet upon a rock, making my steps secure," I saw the light of the Lord in our living room. It glowed all over. When Norm read, "He put a new song in my mouth, a song of praise to our God," I remembered that I had never even heard of the gift of tongues when I first read that Psalm, that night when I was so afraid. I thought of my fear when Dan sat in that room and tried to talk to me about faith. Norm finished with the words that have been proved to me over and over from Psalm 100: "For the Lord is good; his steadfast love endures for ever, and his faithfulness to all generations."

The sun was setting as they drove home from the retreat on Sunday, exhausted and exhilarated at the same time. Josh spoke from the front seat. "That shouldn't be called a retreat. It was more like a charge."

The woman on the seat next to Mary spoke to her in a low voice. "Josh was the best one in our group when we charted theological papers. He seemed to grasp the meaning much better than any adult. Do you talk like that at home, about theology and philosophy? Josh seems to understand so much about the meaning of life."

Mary's voice held a wry note. "No, we just live like that." She ignored the cocked head and questioning look. She changed the subject. "Do you know what I'm going to do when I get home? Go right to bed. My brain isn't used to working that hard. The way they come at you with searching questions even when you eat has my mind blown, absolutely completely blown."

Her resolution was not to be carried out. Norman met her at the door. "Boy, am I glad you're home." His brown eyes looked for reassurance as he went on, "Scott got sick Friday just after you left. He started to vomit." Mary's face paled at his words. She knew this was the most dangerous symptom, indicating a buildup of extreme pressure in Scott's head. "He hasn't even been able to keep down water today."

She ran into the living room. She had to catch her breath when she saw her son. Scott was lying on the couch completely still. His face was ashen grey except for his nose and forehead, swollen and white. He looked as if part of his face were filled with water, a balloon about to burst. Blue veins etched themselves through the white of his eyelids and down his nose. Mary sat down on the edge of the couch, reaching for his wrist. Her fingers waited for the slow, steady beat she usually felt. Instead, the movement was weak and thready, barely perceptible. Scott seemed unaware of her touch.

Mary walked into the bathroom without taking off her coat. She opened the door of the medicine cabinet. Her family stood like frozen statues as she put the thermometer under his tongue, sitting with her finger on his pulse as she waited for the mercury to rise. She took it from under his tongue and looked for the slim silver line. She shook her head, put it back under his tongue.

"What is it?" Norm's question was terse.

"96.6°."

"What about his pulse?"

"Forty-eight."

"Is that bad?"

"That's bad."

"Call Dr. Crawford. See if we can get him to Boston tomorrow."

Mary shook her head. He saw the fear on her face. "No, Norm. That might be too late." She walked to the telephone.

She had never heard Dr. Crawford talk so fast. "Call Dr. Levin immediately," he said after she had outlined Scott's symptoms. "Call me back."

It was with a feeling of relief that she heard Dr. Levin's voice. She had never before reached him at his home. "Bring him into St. Luke's. I'll call them and tell them he's on his way. I'll meet you there."

She kept her finger on Scott's pulse as they drove to Milwaukee. His wrist was chilly. The pulse seemed to fade out completely, then reappear, like a radio station faintly received. She was filled with an anger she didn't understand. It drove out all other feeling. She thought of the retreat, the leader who had been explaining one of Tillich's papers, repeating often in an emotionless voice, "Everything is good." As the car raced through the city streets, her finger on her son's pulse, her mind shouted the words at the unsuspecting retreat leader, "Get lost, lady."

Norm carried Scott into the emergency room and laid him on a stretcher. Dr. Levin's voice quieted Mary's fears when he walked in. The doctor injected a syringe full of medicine into Scott's arm. "We call it the magic medicine," he explained as the pink began to tinge the ashen cheeks.

Mary sat by her son's bed all night, and through the next day when Norm arrived back at the hospital. As they drove home she told Norman what the doctor had said. "Dr. Levin said the shunt is absolutely necessary to save Scott's life. The pressure is too intense for him to be able to make the trip to Boston. He said the head hasn't been able to excrete the dye they injected for the arteriogram when he was in the hospital the last time."

"When will they operate?"

Mary breathed a big sigh of relief. She had expected an argument. "Day after tomorrow."

"Do you care if I go to work instead of waiting at the hospital with you? I hate to miss another day when I laid off last weekend."

"No, I don't care. You can take me in when you go to work in the morning. I'll spend the night with Scott. He's disoriented and seems frightened. Maybe if I'm there, he'll be more calm and quiet. It could make a difference in surgery."

Norm's face lit up with a smile when they walked into Scott's room the next day. His son's eyes were wide open. He seemed aware.

"Hi, Scott. How are you doing?"

The dark eyebrows flew together, a protective V above the hazel eyes that looked up at the man standing beside his bed. His voice was cool. "I'm sorry. I don't speak to strangers." He looked at Mary. "And who are you?"

Her voice sounded shocked. "Why, Scott. I'm your mother."

"I'm sorry. I like my old mother better."

She fought down the impulse for foolish laughter. Noticing the small leaflet he held in his hand, she reached out for it. He handed it to her and watched her as she read the words on it.

"Oh, did you have Communion this morning, Scott?"

"Yes. We all did."

"All who, Scott?"

"Oh, the whole group around this bed." He made a sweeping gesture with his hand. "We all had Communion cards. Each one was a little different from the other. It was lovely."

Scott tossed restlessly all day as his mother sat by his bed. The white-coated figures moved relentlessly in and out of the room, their probing needles extracting blood from reluctant arteries. Scott made no protest when the nurse shaved his head, scrubbing it with soap and water, exposing the semicircular scar that ran across the top, from ear to ear.

"Well, good night, nice lady, whoever you are." The voice sounded sleepy. "Thank you for keeping me company all day today. I hope I can do the same for you someday."

Mary sat by her son's bed, Bible in her hands. Scott's eyes opened as the light began to filter in through the window. He looked at his mother.

"Mother, what are you doing here so early?"

"I stayed all night, Scott."

"Didn't you get any sleep?"

"I'm all right."

He looked around the room. "Why am I in the hospital?"

"Dr. Levin is going to put in a shunt today."

"Why?"

"Fluid is accumulating in your head in the cavities where the tumor was removed. He's going to put a tube from your brain down into your heart, to drain off the fluid that's causing pressure. You'll be all right again then."

"Good. We knew there was something really wrong, didn't we? I'm glad they're going to fix it. I want to go back to school. I want to learn how to be a doctor." He looked at the book in his mother's hand. "Read me a Psalm, will you, Mother?"

Mary wrote in her journal two weeks later.

Scott is out of the hospital. Recovery is slow. Dr. Levin said it would be. He said he wouldn't spring back in ten days like he did the first time. Scott sleeps most of the time.

We received some mail on Huntington's disease from Marjorie Guthrie. I was thinking of the time when Josh was in grade school. He walked home. He told me he was singing his favorite song all the way home, "This land is my land, this land is your land." I could just hear him singing the lines when I opened the mail from Marjorie Guthrie. How strange that we would be involved in the same disease as the writer of that song, Woody Guthrie. Marjorie Guthrie has started a Committee to Combat Huntington's Disease, at Suite 2016, 250 W. 57th St., New York, New York. I am going to write to her. They plan to start some family counseling. I'm going to find out about that.

Norm has been spending more time away from home again. I had thought maybe now that we found out what was wrong with Scott, he would stay away from the taverns. I guess I thought wrong. I guess I'll go to bed. I've been sitting here on the couch, waiting for Norm to come home. No sense sitting any longer.

CHAPTER SIXTEEN

THE DOMINO EFFECT

Mary held the dustpan on the floor as she swept up the pile of dirt in the kitchen the next morning. She straightened, rubbing her back, looking around the room and into the living room to see if they would meet the inspecting eyes she expected to come down the stairs soon.

Norman spoke to his wife as she took the pie from the oven. The juice oozed from the slits in the top in thick, pink trickles. "Umm, apple pie. Can I have a piece?"

"For breakfast?"

"Why not?" He walked to the cupboard and opened the door. "Where are all the cups?"

"In the dishwasher. I haven't had a chance to put them away yet."

Norm rubbed his index finger inside a cup. "Is that dishwasher broken again? This cup isn't clean. It's covered with scum."

"Oh, it's been acting kind of strange. I've been meaning to tell you."

His eyebrows flew together. His voice rose in imitation of hers. "Kind of strange, kind of strange. That makes a lot of sense. Nobody ever tells me anything around here. No wonder the whole place is falling apart."

"Well, you don't spend much time at home preventing it, do you? Where were you last night?"

"That's right. Blame me. Everything is always my fault."

"Well, I'm no plumber."

"That's right, you sure aren't. You're a lousy money manager too, I can tell you that." He took out his checkbook and waved it in front of his wife, who stood by the sink, hands on her hips. He ran his finger down the lines at the edge of the checks. "Look at this—'cash, Mary; cash, Mary; cash, Mary.' What do you *do* with all the money I give you?"

"Spend it on myself. I buy new clothes, new shoes, new coats, of course," Mary said sarcastically. "How many checks in there are made out to the liquor store?"

Norman advanced on her, his face reddening. He pointed his right index finger. "You're crazy. That's what you are, you're crazy."

Mary walked toward the back door. She turned as she reached it, her eyes dark. "That's right. I must be. I must be crazy to listen to you talk to me like that. I know one thing, I'm getting out of here before I go completely insane."

The car seemed to point itself. It drove through the town, out the highway, then drove down the Swansons' long drive. The trees and bushes celebrated the season in shades of red and yellow. Mary drove up the hill toward the big white house and parked in front of the garage. She got out of the car and went to sit down on the big stump at the top of the hill, behind the garage, hidden from the house. The breeze whipped whitecaps on the lake. Peninsula fingers of green on the other shoreline formed a picture frame for the family of wood ducks that glided across the water, a ballet with the music of the wind. Mary sat very still, absorbing the peace.

Karen Swanson's voice greeted her when she walked into the big front porch. "Why, Mary, am I glad to see you. How's Scott?" Mary looked at the attractive dark-haired mother who stood in the doorway to the hall, holding her brown-eyed boy in her arms. She noticed that the porch, used as a nursery for the meetings, was noisy with children playing with all the toys.

"Fine, thank you. He's getting stronger slowly."

"Wonderful. I'm so glad you came out this morning. I've been hoping you would start coming to Bible study on Wednesday mornings. In fact, I've been praying that you would."

Mary felt trapped. She followed the young woman in the brightly printed slacks and shirt. Karen handed her a Bible as she sat down in the blue leather chair beside the fireplace. Mary looked around the circle of faces. She recognized none.

Karen smiled at her, her eyes warm, her mouth dimpled at the corners. "We're studying 1 Peter 3 this morning."

Mary leafed through the Bible she held. She read through the first few verses. "Likewise, ye wives, be in subjection to your own husbands; that, if any obey not the word, they also may without the word be won by the conversation of the wives." She felt betrayed. Her mind shouted, "Oh no! How can you do this to me, God?" Her memory flashed back to the scene in her kitchen as she heard the women discuss the chapter, apparently in full agreement.

"OK," her voice broke into the quiet circle. "Let me tell you what brought me out here this morning."

As she talked, Karen got up and left the room. She came back in with a box of tissues in her hand. She handed Mary one. She stood rubbing Mary's back as Mary put her hands over her face, her shoulders shuddering.

"That isn't fair. That really isn't fair." It was the short woman they had introduced as Grandma Kay who spoke up. "I had to learn not to answer at all when my husband was angry. That was the only way that worked for me. You know," she went on, as if to give Mary time to regain her composure, "I had an old Norwegian aunt who used to say, 'It may be the husband who's the head of the house, but the wife is the neck. You know what happens to the head when the neck turns?' "

The house was quiet when Mary walked in. Norman was sound asleep in the chair in the corner of the living room. There was an empty beer bottle beside his chair. Mary went to the cupboard where she kept her journal. She walked up the stairs and sat on her bed.

> I'm glad I went to Swansons' this morning. I'm glad I had to read that chapter in 1 Peter. I have to realize I'm not going to change Norman. The only person I can change is Mary. I have to stop expecting more of Norman than he can give me. I have to realize he'll always want me to be more than I can be. He can't help the way he's going, at least not until he asks God to help him. I'll have to stop being so sensitive. I can't get my feelings hurt so easily. I must stop getting mad. So we don't talk. Is that so important, really? Norm doesn't care if I talk to other people. Dan talked to me. Where is Dan now, Mary?

After school that day, Josh stood in front of the refrigerator, holding the door open, peering inside the lighted cavity.

"Josh," Mary said, "I'm glad to have a chance to talk with you before your father gets home. Your guidance counselor called from school today. He said your grades are slipping badly."

"I don't care. I hate school."

"But, Josh, you'll never get anywhere if you don't go to school." They both heard the car in the driveway.

Nobody said a word all during supper. As Josh got up to leave the table, his father grabbed him by the shirt-sleeve. "When are you going to get that hair cut?"

Josh pulled his arm away with a jerk, walked to the door of the basement, and opened it. He took his jacket off the hook.

"Where do you think you're going?" Mary caught her breath as her husband stood up, blocking the way out of the kitchen.

"I said, when are you going to get your hair cut? I expect an answer."

She hadn't noticed how tall Josh was growing until he stood almost nose to nose with his father. Their eyes dueled, an even match in shade and feeling.

The muscles of Josh's jaw clenched in little knots, then shot out the words through teeth almost touching. "It's my hair."

Norm raised a clenched fist. Mary jumped up and grabbed his arm. "Norm, don't hit him. Don't hit him."

Josh slammed the door with a defiant bang as he left the house. Norm glared at his wife, then went upstairs.

Mary hung up the phone several hours later with a sigh of relief. She had been very glad to give Josh permission to spend the night with a friend, especially one whose mother she knew rather well.

She had another phone call the next day. It was almost as if she had been expecting what she heard. She wasn't really surprised.

"Mary, you knew Josh stayed here last night, didn't you?"

"Yes, Dana, I did. He called to let me know where he was."

"I hate to hand you more problems than you already have. I know what a worry Scott's condition has been. But I think you ought to know what I found in Josh's cigarette case this morning."

"What?"

"I'm a very nosy person. When I saw the cigarette case on the floor of Lew's bedroom where they slept, I thought, 'I wonder what kind of cigarettes he smokes. That's an awfully short case.' When I opened it, I didn't find any cigarettes. There was a little brown packet of something that smells kind of strange. I assume it's marijuana."

"Where is it now?"

"In my purse. You can have it if you want it."

"I have to go downtown this morning. I'll stop and get it."

After her husband came home, she waited until he had opened his first can of beer. Then she told him.

"Where is it?"

"In my top drawer."

"What did Josh say?"

"I didn't tell him anything about it yet. He doesn't know I have it."

"We'd better talk to Charlie. Maybe he'd know what to do."

"I already did. I stopped at the church after I picked up the cigarette case. He said we should report Josh to the District Attorney."

"Oh, I don't know about that."

"That's the way I feel. Charlie said we need to make the kids face their responsibilities; we need to support the law."

"Is that the way he talks to all the adults in his church? How about the ones who welsh on their income taxes? Does he report them to the DA?"

"He didn't say he'd report Josh. He said we should. He said that's what several other families in church have done, and it seems to be working out all right. He said the DA is fair to the kids. He just tries to find out where they're getting the stuff."

"That seems to me an admission that we can't handle our own son."

"I have a suggestion. I think we should go for help. There's a man in the clinic where Dan used to work. I've met him. I liked him a lot. He's a Catholic priest who works with drug addiction and alcoholism. I could try to get an appointment with him."

Mary was grateful they could get an appointment for the next day and that Norman agreed to go. She had expected they would have to wait longer.

The priest shook hands firmly. Mary noted the contrast

between him and her husband as they talked. Instead of Norm's baldness, his dark hair was greying at the temple. His long, tapered fingers played with a pencil. His attitude was relaxed and easy. It seemed to emphasize Norm's posture. Norm sat on the edge of his chair, his hands on his knees, as if crouched and ready to spring. His powerful shoulders looked very broad as Mary glanced from Norman to the tall, slim, black-robed figure. She guessed they were about the same age. Norm's face, tanned and ruddy from exposure to the weather as he walked the length of the freight trains, showed none of the emotion he must be feeling as he talked with the man whose white skin spoke of asceticism to Mary's imagination.

"Have you talked with the boy about what you found?"

"Yes." Mary spoke quickly. "I was proud of the way Norm handled it. He told Josh he should become a lawyer and work for the legalization of marijuana, or a doctor and study the effects of drugs. I never would have thought of that."

"Good." The psychologist nodded. "You are saying, then, that you didn't get angry when you talked with him."

"I was mad. But I knew it wouldn't do any good if I let Josh know that," Norm explained.

Dr. Cy Boda smiled. "That's an honest answer, but you're right about that. It would have done a lot of harm."

Mary spoke up. "I talked with our minister about it. He said we should report Josh to the District Attorney. Neither of us thought that would be the right thing to do."

"That would have been one of the worst things you could have done. That probably would have alienated Josh completely."

Norm nodded at Mary. He smiled at the priest. "Right."

"You're going to have to make up your minds that you're in for a rough time for quite a while with Josh. The kind of behavior you've been describing," the priest told them after they had talked about a half-hour about their second son, "is a typical pattern for a young person who's trying to find an escape for his pain. Josh's problem is undoubtedly connected with Scott's. You have both been so deeply affected by what has happened to your oldest son that you couldn't notice what was happening with your other children. You can expect a domino effect. Now that Scott is better, Josh can begin to show his needs. You might find the same pattern developing in the other children. With Josh, I'm quite sure it will get worse before it gets better. But it will get better. Please keep that in mind. Josh has had enough love and security in his beginning years that he will be able to sort it all out. Your problem is probably going to be in allowing him to do so. You will have to give him the freedom to fail, allowing him the responsibility for living his own life, even when it's not the kind of life you wish he were living. Do you think you can do that?"

"I like him." Norm spoke to Mary as he turned on the ignition.

"I like him too. I like him a lot. I hope Josh will go and talk with him. Do you think he will?"

"I don't know. But remember what he said. You can't push him."

"I know. What was it he said—Josh would have to have readiness?"

"That was it. Readiness. Do you know he wouldn't even let me pay him anything? If we had gone to a psychiatrist, that would have cost us fifty dollars!"

Two days later Mary wrote in her journal.

> Josh came home from school today sick. He was out late last night. When he came home, I took advantage of the quiet house to have a talk with him. I told him I thought he had a problem, that he needs help. He said he didn't want to talk about it. I remembered what Dr. Boda had said, and let it go.

A week later she wrote again.

I got up early. I couldn't sleep. It was a beautiful meeting last night. A real lifesaver. I needed it. Norm got his check yesterday. He went down to the bank, taking Becca with him. They were gone four hours. Becca told me when she came home, they had been at Red's. She said she hates to go there. She told me some old man kept trying to buy her candy bars that she didn't want. I was so disappointed and hurt. I asked Norm why he went. He said, "I did it because you threatened me the other day." I asked him how I had threatened him. He said, "You told me you were so glad that I had quit drinking, because if I hadn't quit, it would have wrecked our marriage." I said I didn't call that a threat. He looked at me, his brows lowering, and said, "I call that a threat. Nobody threatens me." I just walked away. I simply have to turn this problem over to God. I must take my mind off it. I must not worry. I cannot react. Please, Lord, help me do what I know with my head is what I have to do. It's so hard when I am feeling emotional. Help me not to be so emotional, please, please, God.

CHAPTER SEVENTEEN

CONFRONTATION

Mary's journal gave evidence in the next several months of the turmoil that was beginning to engulf the entire family.

February 23

Josh didn't come home after school yesterday. About eleven last night, I was so worried about him that I took Scott down to Red's to see if we could find Norm. Norm was terribly mean. I should have left him in the tavern. I'm never going to do that again.

Today a very important truth broke through to me, one I have never before realized: I am responsible for only one immortal soul, mine. God will draw these others to himself, as he drew me. If I get too anxious about it, it will only do harm. The best thing I can do is to turn my entire family over to him. God loves them all more than I love them. God loves Norman.

I am very grateful that Norm is willing to share me to the extent that he is sharing me. He seems to have given up his distrust of my going to the Friday night meetings at Swansons', thank God. If I couldn't go, I just might lose my sanity. It is only in complete freedom of worship that I myself can be fully free. It's just as if in raising my arms and praising the Lord, I'm giving my burdens to him. He takes them. The next time Norm gets mean, they come back on me, but at least I know I have somewhere to go to find full release. Thank you, Lord.

It seems to me that I've been an ungrateful daughter of my heavenly Father. I've trusted him so little. I've believed his Word with such little faith. Talk about a grain of mustard seed—mine has been an atom. But just as power is released when the tiniest particle of matter, the atom, is split, so it is with the children of God. When we can trust him enough to allow him to split us wide open, to be totally vulnerable to him, to his Word, to his ministry through other worshiping Christians, then wow! What he can begin to do with us! I don't totally grasp this yet; it's just beginning to become clear to me. That shows another area in my lack of faith, the rejection of the idea of speaking in tongues, so that I didn't even want the gift. God had to give it to me. He knew my need even if I did not.

God, we are a stubborn and a hard-hearted people. We read your Word, but we don't fully believe it. We have to get our own heads in it, to interpret it for ourselves, instead of taking it at face value. What you say you will do, you do. It's as simple as that. O Lord, O God, help me to learn the lessons you are trying to teach me. Help me to in some way tell others so they won't have to go through all this hell.

May 3

Scott called from school last week. He said he had been having muscle spasms and was feeling nauseated. I called Dr. Levin. He said we should get the visual fields checked. We had the fields done on Wednesday, then took them right over to Dr. Levin. He said the range of vision was much smaller, probably indicating regrowth of the tumor. Scott has been telling me for several weeks that he can't see very well anymore. He said he can't see when he looks to either side, only straight ahead. We picked Josh up on the way home from the doctor's office; he was

walking home from school. I told him what the doctor had said. Josh said, "When I saw the car, I knew
you were going to tell me the tumor is growing
again." Norm didn't say one word when I told him.
If he starts drinking excessively again, I think it
might kill our marriage. But I must not even consider
that. It's in God's hands. He's the Father. I'm Scott's
mother. I'm not Norm's mother. I'm so thankful the
Lord revealed that concept to me. I thank God he told
me, "You are responsible only for your own soul. I'll
take care of the rest."

May 7

I was looking in Josh's dresser drawers the other
day for any evidence of dope. Humiliating thing to
do. Humiliating to Josh's image in my mind, and to
my image of myself. But I do it anyway. I didn't find
any dope. I did find this poem.

soft edges of clouds under moonlight
black storm clouds flying by
green fish in black water gulping moonlight
silver moonlight in black night shining from the
    water
twirling, swirling, smoking light, dancing down
ink dropped in water
wind weaving fields of tall grass
jungles of grass leaping, jumping, swaying in unison
skipping grass blown by the wind
raising dust
bringing rain clouds chasing schools of death
hurricanes of death
grey death
white coldness
green life springing
windblown water
green waving water melting into moonlight

whirling, twirling, swaying, conjuring
dancing moonlight dancing from the water
dancing from the earth
laughing, prancing, loving, hating, defying, relying.
who am I?
where am I?
where do I go?
what do I do?

God, the imagery tears at my heart. Help him, Lord. I don't know how.

What relationship does this have with his use of dope? What relationship does it have with his father's use of alcohol? What relationship does it have with what's happening in his brother's head? What kind of help can I give him? All I can think of to do, God, is to pray. I ask you to help him. I don't know how.

Scott spent only one day in school last week. Tuesday the school called and asked me to come and get him. The counselor said he had been sleeping more and more. He has an almost constant headache. I've had to start giving him the pitressin shots that we phased out several years ago when the diabetes insipidus subdued. He was wetting the bed almost nightly, urinating copiously during the day.

That tumor just has to be growing. What else would be doing all this? His coordination is going also.

The hospital fired Scott. I'm almost glad. I was so afraid he was going to blow his top and spoil his good relationships. He's getting less able to control his temper once it gets going. Becca flinches every time he yells at her. I think she's afraid of him.

Mary put her journal away as Gretchen came into the kitchen. Gretchen looked surprised as her mother walked over and hugged her tightly.

"Gretch, you're a good girl."

"Why, Mother, why do you say that?"

"Because you and Heidi never make me worry. I was reading the Bible the other night, about children honoring their parents. I think you honor your parents, Gretch. So does Heidi."

"Dad wouldn't say that, Mother. He says we're the messiest slobs he's ever seen."

"He doesn't really mean that, Gretch. I know he's proud of you."

"He doesn't act like he is, Mom."

Becca came running into the kitchen, screaming loudly. She grabbed Gretchen's legs, burying her face as Scott came running after her. His face was red. His fist was raised. He tugged at the little arm that fastened onto her sister's leg even more tightly.

"Scott, Scott, let her go, let her go."

Mary took hold of his arm. He released his sister. He turned toward his mother. His clenched fist went up. His hand shook. It stopped inches from her face.

Mary looked her son in the eyes. Her voice was soft. "Scott. Stop it. Put your hand down."

Scott opened his mouth as he lowered his fist. He voiced his feelings in a shout of wordless fury. He turned and ran out of the kitchen, through the living room, and out the front door. Mary watched him run down the walk and disappear down the road, pounding small clouds of dust into the air with each step. She picked up the little girl who was whimpering softly against her sister's legs. She held her on her lap until she relaxed, singing soft songs to quiet her.

"OK." Her mother stood up and put Becca down on the floor. She patted her seat and said, "Run along outside and play."

Mary walked to the bookcase in the living room and took out the Bible. She sat down on the couch and began to read.

Soon Scott came through the front door smiling, a startling contrast to his expression an hour earlier.

"Mother, do you know what happened? I ran down the road until I got to the big maple tree. I sat down under the tree and asked God to take my temper away. I asked him to make me get over being mad at you and Becca. He did. I got all filled up with peace and joy, so I stood up to come home. Then I remembered that I hadn't thanked God for answering my prayer, so I sat down again. I said, 'Thank you, God, for answering my prayer.' Then, Mother, guess what happened?"

"What, Scott?"

"I felt something touch my shoulder. I opened up my eyes and looked up. It was an angel." He nodded his head as he smiled. "Yes, I saw an angel."

"An angel? What did it look like?"

"It had a big smile on its face which shone all over with a sort of rosy pinky glow. It was really beautiful. It was neither male nor female. It looked sort of like a feather mermaid, but the feathers were wisps of air. It kind of drifted off into nothingness." He sighed deeply. "It was really beautiful."

Mary didn't know what to say. She looked at the Bible she had been reading when he came in the room. "Well, there were quite a few people in here who saw angels."

"I know." His nod was confident. "Do you know what I was thinking about when I was walking home, Mother?"

"No, Scott. What?"

"About Dan. And how much I've missed him."

"Have you missed him, Scott? You've never talked about him since he left."

"That's 'cause I've missed him so much. When he and I used to go out in his car and pray, Mother, it was like being with an angel sent to me. But now God has sent me a real angel. Isn't God good to me, Mother?"

"Yes, Scott. He really is. Think of all the wonderful doctors he has given you too."

"That's right. Didn't you say we were going to see Dr. Levin soon?"

"Tomorrow."

Mary sat across from the doctor's desk, on the couch where she could look out the window over the roofs of the city buildings to Lake Michigan. She watched the smoke drift away from a big steamer, trying not to anticipate what the doctor would say. He had suggested she step into his office while Scott was dressing. She heard the door open.

"Mrs. Soergel," he began as he sat down at his desk, "there are no clinical manifestations of the tumor because it is growing invasively, not obstructively as it grew previously."

Mary willed her mind to organize the questions that had been running rampant in her head. She tried to concentrate on what the doctor was saying as her heart started pounding hard.

"I don't have a very cheerful prognosis." He paused for a moment, looking into her face, his eyes serious.

She hit her feelings head on. "How long does he have to live?"

"Two to five years. But that isn't the biggest problem. The biggest problem is what will happen during that period of time. Scott will gradually lose all control of his emotions. There will come a time when he will probably have to be institutionalized."

"But where?"

"That's the problem. Nobody wants these people. I would hate to see him in Southern Colony."

"How about his intelligence? Will that go too?"

"Probably not. The part of Scott's brain that controls his intellect isn't involved. That's what makes it so difficult. He still has a very keen intelligence. He realizes what's happening to him. I could tell by his questions. His memory, emotional control, organizational ability are going, but he still thinks very clearly. That would be the most difficult part of putting him into an institution that cares for only the most severely retarded. He's so aware."

Scott slept all the way home. Mary's mind was on the advertisement that had been catching her eye in the local paper for almost a year. The only factor that had prevented her from checking into it was the price tag. She shuffled through the pile of papers on the small table in the living room after she got home, and read the ad again.

> 80 acres with creek and fish pond. Large four-bedroom home. Barn and other outbuildings. $55,000.

She said the phone number over to herself as she picked up the phone.

Her stomach fluttered the next day as she watched out the kitchen window for the real estate salesman who had sounded delighted to show her the farm. When she came home, she was glad to see her husband's car in the driveway. She began to talk as soon as she walked in the door. That night she again wrote in her journal.

> I'm so excited that I have to write about the beautiful farm I just saw. No advertisement could possibly describe it. It has a stream that meanders from the front of the property to the back in swooping curves. There's a pond just the right size for swimming, fishing, skating. There are hills for skiing and tobogganing. There are several springs that gurgle out fresh water. The house is nice. It has beautiful, shiny hardwood floors. I have always loved hardwood floors. But what really sold me is the basement. There's one big, long room on the north end with really thick stone walls, with its own outside entrance. If Dr. Levin is right and Scott will have to be locked up, we can lock him up there.
>
> Scott's temp is becoming very erratic. It shoots way, way up. It was 102.6° this morning. When his

temp goes up, so does his temper. We could make him a nice bedroom workshop in that big basement room.

One thing I know for sure. I don't know how long God has for Scott to live. That's God's business, not mine. But how Scott lives out those years is my business. I know for certain that his heavenly Father who loves him will help me keep him out of an institution, if I ask. I'm asking right now. Please, God. Give us that farm.

Mary put her journal away, but she didn't put the farm out of her mind. On the way out to Swansons' she determined to ask for prayers in the meeting that was scheduled an hour ahead of the general prayer meeting, where a great number of people would seek help with gut-level problems.

After they had gone into the den, Mary told the circle of sympathetic faces what the doctor had said about Scott. She told them about the farm, trying to describe the strange conviction that she had felt that morning that this was supposed to be their farm, in spite of the frightening price tag. They all knew that the accumulation of medical bills made money a big problem; she had shared that often enough. Jack lifted a chair into the middle of the circle. Mary sat down in it. They placed their hands on her shoulders as they each prayed in the private prayer language God had given them.

Karen's brown eyes shone as she looked at her friend when they had finished. "You know, Mare, this may be really far-out, but while we prayed, a thought flashed through my head. I know of a fund that has quite a bit of money to invest. Sometimes they invest it in land. I'll give you the name of the chairman of the board. Call him. Maybe they could help you out by buying part of the farm as an investment."

At nine the next morning, Mary dialed the number

Karen had given her. The voice on the other end of the line sounded nice, but dubious, when she told him why she was calling. She hung up the phone with a feeling of futility. The phone rang as she walked away from it. The voice of Tricia, the girl she had never met in person, asked for Josh. She stayed in the kitchen listening as they talked, remembering the previous sleepless night. When he hung up the phone, she burst out at him, a fountain of words. "Josh, that girl is no good for you. I don't think you should see her anymore. Everybody tells me just awful things about her. How do you think I felt last night waiting until 3:30 for you to get home, wondering if you were killed along the highway somewhere?"

Josh flinched as if she had hit him. He blinked his eyes and walked out of the room.

Mary felt a little ashamed of her outburst as she ran the dishwasher. When she had finished the dishes, she started to sweep the floor. Josh came into the room, his jacket on. He handed his mother the large, yellow-lined sheets of paper that he held in his hand. She saw the big printed words; the letters were purple. Josh walked out the back door as his mother leaned the broom against the counter, sat down on the stool by the phone, and read.

> Sometimes people have to be separated to come together again. When you can't talk, or your true feelings are not coming across, it is separation. When people are denied this right for any reason (in this case so many complex ones), something has to be done. The best things are the hardest things to come by. This is life. Life is living and learning. When you are not doing that, you are nowhere. When told not to go out to live and learn, it ends up horribly. This is not to say there is no faith or hope. Trust can be reestablished, in this case obviously only the hard way.
>
> Love,
> Josh

Mary walked up the stairs, taking them two at a time. She threw herself down on her bed, her mind a whirling storm of emotion. She pounded her fist on the bedspread. "God, you are going to have to help me. I don't know what to do. Please, God. Who can get through to this boy? Who will he listen to?"

She almost heard the word pronounced. "Tricia."

"But God," she was whispering now, "I've been so rude to her when she calls. How can I ask her to help me?" The silence answered her. She got up off the bed and walked to the phone. She picked up the phone book. She dialed. The phone rang and rang. She went back into the room and flopped down on the bed.

She said aloud, "Now what, God?"

"Mother," Heidi's voice called up the stairs, "Tricia's down here. She wants to see you."

Mary couldn't believe her ears. She ran down the stairs. She stood on the bottom step, looking down at this girl she had never seen before. She was not as she had imagined her to be. She was very small. Mary received a quick impression of Dresden china fragility in oversize overalls. Her light brown hair curled over her head in a fine mist. Her eyes were very blue and very big.

Mary reached for the hand that felt delicate and fine-boned. "Oh, Tricia, I'm so glad to see you. Come on upstairs. I have to talk to you. Josh is gone."

They sat on the bed. Mary's detached self watched the scene. She was aware that this was a new experience for Tricia. She realized that her own suspicions were crumbling as she poured out her feelings about Josh, grateful that there was another person who truly cared what happened to him. Mary showed her the yellow paper with big purple words. She read it in silence. The big blue eyes looked sad.

"Where is he now?"

"I don't know." Mary shook her head. She put the handkerchief to her eyes.

"I'll go find him." Tricia got off the bed. She shrugged into the damp overall jacket she had dropped to the floor when she came into the bedroom.

"I'll take you downtown. It's cold and rainy," Mary offered.

"No, I'll walk."

When she walked out the front door, Mary watched the small back disappear down the road.

Two weeks later, only the light above the kitchen table lit the still house as Mary wrote in her journal, waiting for her husband.

> The fund man called today. He said the committee had decided against investing in the farm. I wasn't too surprised. I still have the feeling this is our farm. Please, God.

The barking of the dog outside the house interrupted her thoughts. She stuffed the journal back in the cupboard as she heard the car door slam. She picked up the newspaper and spread it out on the table.

"What are you doing up?" Norm asked.

"Waiting for you. The man called about investing in the farm land today. He said the finance committee had met and rejected the idea."

Norm put down the beer he carried. He hung his jacket over the back of the chair.

"Maybe it's just as well. I've been wanting to talk to you about that anyway." He pulled a can away from the circle of plastic and held it toward his wife. "Want a beer?"

She shook her head.

He sat down at the table. "How would you feel about looking for a farm near Portage?"

Mary looked at him, her eyebrows raised. She held her breath as he continued, apparently unaware of how she felt. "The railroad is thinking of changing divisions, making them longer. If they do, mine will run from Portage to

Chicago. I would end up in Portage. I think it would be much better to look for a farm there. It would be cheaper too. Taxes wouldn't be so high. I've known they were considering it for a long time, but I didn't want to tell you. I was afraid you might be upset."

Mary's stomach had tightened into a knot as her husband talked. She realized he wanted to move. She felt as if she couldn't breathe deeply enough to take in enough air. Her hands were suddenly very cold.

"Well, what do you think? Why don't you say something?"

"I'm sorry, Norm. I don't know what I think. I've never even considered moving away from here. What about Scott?"

"What do you mean, what about Scott?"

"He would be about two hours farther away from Dr. Levin."

"I told you to take Scott back to Dr. Crawford. I don't believe Dr. Levin. I have never believed Dr. Levin. Didn't Dr. Crawford say last time you talked with him that he doesn't think the brain tumor has recurred?"

"Yes."

"Well, there you are. Scott could get to Boston out of Portage as well as he can from here. He could fly from Madison."

Mary closed her eyes, shaking her head from side to side. She stood up. "I'm going to bed. I'll think about it."

As his wife walked toward the dining room, Norm tossed the empty beer can into the wastebasket just inside the door. It hit hard against the side of the wastebasket with a defiant bang. Mary turned back toward her husband who had picked up the newspaper. He looked at her across the top of the page, his eyes narrowing as she asked, "If the brain tumor isn't growing back, what is causing Scott's violent behavior? Why did he get so mad at me today that he jabbed his fist at me? If Josh hadn't grabbed him, he would have hit me."

The words shot out at him, angry bullets against the shield of newspaper that he raised higher as she talked, until his eyes were hidden from her. Silence her only reply, Mary swiveled on her foot and ran toward the stairs.

Her mood was as grey as the November day as she drove down the long winding drive toward the big brick monastery. The little lake resisted the wind with small whitecaps that came up for a breath of air, then sank back under the cold water. The branches of the willow trees along the banks drooped long, cold fingers, then blew a chilly greeting to her as she slammed the door of the car and walked up the steps. She sensed silent disapproval in the stern face of the old man who answered her ring. He directed her to Dr. Boda's apartment with a voice devoid of expression. Mary felt very self-conscious as she walked down the hall, passing the curious eyes under the black hoods. She noted Cy left the door ajar after he led her into his apartment. She forgot her momentary discomfort as he lifted a stack of books off the soft chair beside the low table, also piled high with books.

"Excuse the mess, Mary. I've been writing all week. I haven't bothered to pick up one thing."

"What are you writing?"

"A book on communication."

"Wow. I'll buy the first one. That's the biggest problem in my marriage."

"It is in most marriages, Mary. That's why I'm writing, for people like you and Norm. What brings you out here today?"

His eyes seemed to penetrate so deeply into her feelings that she suddenly had an uncontrollable surge of tears. She reached into the pocket of her sweater. Cy handed her a white handkerchief. It smelled faintly of lemon as she put it over her face. She shook her head.

"I'm sorry, Cy."

"Mary," the voice scolded softly, "why do you always

say you're sorry? Don't you think you're allowed to have feelings?"

She lifted her hands, palms outstretched in a gesture of bewilderment.

"I don't know, Cy," she whispered. "I don't know why I cry, and I don't know why I think I shouldn't cry."

He laughed a little. "Well, what do you know, Mary? Why did you come? What do you want to talk about?" His voice lowered compassionately as he saw her struggling to stop the tears. "How can I help you, Mary? How can I help?"

"Cy, I realized last night..." She hesitated, swallowed, then went on rapidly, "I couldn't sleep all night. I suddenly knew last night that my security is no longer in my marriage." She shook her head. The hazel eyes that usually reflected the colors she wore mirrored her pain in shades of grey, turning her eyes almost black.

"Mary, maybe your security never was in your marriage. You just never realized it before. Most people have such an idealized picture of marriage in their minds that they can be married for years and years and still think the person they married is all the things they have always pictured their mate as being—understanding, strong, loving, sharing, unselfish. It's only when a crisis such as you have lived with comes to a marriage that the strength, or weakness, shows up."

Mary wrote about her conversation with the priest in her journal that night, after the children were in bed.

> It really helped me to talk it out. Cy never advises. He simply helps me understand how I really feel, not how I think I should feel. He also tells me predictable behavior patterns, so that I know what to anticipate. I thank God for Cy.
>
> I am going to share with our Saturday morning prayer group what Cy said. That group seems to be really getting it together. We have been using a book that Charlie recommended, *Two or Three Together,* by Harold Freer and Frances Hall. They define a prayer group as "a small, intimate comradeship, united in a

common commitment which through regular group discipline seeks spiritual power and direction." So it is a good thing that we are only six. I have shared everything with them. They are really praying for Josh and Norm. At first we spent too much time talking; so now when we come in, we come in silence, sit on the floor for a half hour meditating, reading, whatever—we all do our own thing. I am wondering if Dan hadn't left, if he would have joined this group? Forget it, Mary.

Lord God, after getting it straightened out in my head, after talking with Cy, I know I can't leave here. I know where my real strength is. It's in the body of Christ. I have such a different concept of the body of Christ than I did formerly. I used to think of it as my own denominational church. I know now that it is much more than that, although that's an important part. It's also in the Christian community I've found at Swansons'. It's in Cy's generous sharing of himself, with his wisdom and immediate availability. It's in the choir that surrounds me every Sunday when we sing. How many times have their voices sustained me with the words I needed to hear, when I couldn't sing for the tears in my throat? These are the forces that keep me going. I know that if I were in Portage, with Norm in some phoneless tavern, me with no car, and Scott exploding out in the country on some strange farm with four other children who would have all the problems that transplanting them would cause, I'd crack up. I'm not all that strong. So, God, you'll have to work it out. You know my limitations. You know me better than I know myself. You know I want to stay married to Norman. Please help me accept Norm as he is, not as I wish he were. You know I want to live on the farm you've already picked out for us. I trust you, God. You work it all out. I can't. Thank you.

CHAPTER EIGHTEEN

WILLA DORSEY SINGS

Mary sat at the kitchen table. In her hand she held the cassette that Karen had lent her. There was an irritated frown on her face as she pulled out the tape and reinserted it in the slot. She looked up as her husband came through the kitchen on his way to work.

"Norm, take this thing along with you, please, and see if you can get it going for me. Karen's mother sent me a tape of Willa Dorsey. Karen was raving about her singing last time she came home from visiting her mom. She lent me her player, but I can't make it work."

The next night she was cleaning up the kitchen after all the children were in bed.

"Mary!" Norm's voice was excited as he came through the back door. "You have to listen to this. I listened to this tape all the way home." He thumped the six-pack down on the table, sat down without taking off his coat, and turned on the cassette. As the piano played softly, he looked up at his wife, his brown eyes deep with feeling.

"You have to hear this. It got me right here." He clutched at his chest. The popping sound of his opening a beer can was drowned by the voice that spoke out in a high clear soprano:

"Jesus walks with me and he talks with me when I let him have his own way in my life. I challenge you tonight, let God have his way. Don't tell him what to do for you, how to do it, when to do it. You can't order him around, you know. His thoughts and his ways are as far from ours as the earth is from the sky. Ask him tonight to have his way in your life. He will hear you, if you let him have his way."

Mary watched her husband with amazement as he pulled the tape from the machine, reinserted it, and played it over three times without taking even one sip of the can of beer that sat between him and the cassette.

He turned to look at his wife, who was sitting on the stool by the pass-through into the dining room. "Well, what do you think, Mare?"

"I think she has a beautiful voice."

"No, no. I mean, what do you think about what she said?"

"Do you mean about letting God have his way in your life?"

"Yes, that's what I mean."

"She's right, Norm, she's right."

They listened to Willa's album Christmas day at Swansons' after dinner. The coals glowing in the fireplace seemed to reflect the light that filled the room and shone from their faces as they watched Krista and David Swanson play on the floor with their new Christmas toys.

"Norm, that was a fantastic roast you cooked for us." Karen's voice was warm as she looked across the fireplace to the big chair in the corner where Norm sat, holding Becca on his lap.

"Thanks, Karen." The corners of his eyes crinkled as Norm smiled. "I've never cooked such a big roast on a rotisserie before. It did taste pretty good."

Jack patted his stomach. "It was more than pretty good. That was the best tasting Christmas present anybody ever gave me. Thanks, Norm."

Jack looked at Scott, who fought to keep his eyes open as the warmth of the fire toasted the sweater Karen had given him. "What was the best present you got this Christmas, Scott?"

"Life."

Karen's voice broke into the sobered silence. She put her hand on the shoulder of the boy who was beginning to show traces of the man he would become. His lengthening legs were crossed as he sat on the floor, helping David put his new erector set together. "What about you, Josh?"

Josh reached into his pocket. He pulled out a folded sheet of lined paper. He handed it to Karen, then directed his attention quickly back to the tower he and David were building together. Karen scanned the words quickly "Josh, this is beautiful. May I share it?"

Josh nodded without raising his eyes.

> Yahweh gives me his blood and flesh and water
> To make me born in Yahweh love.
> I was in a pit with worms.
> Fear was stuck inside like tar.
> My enemy made me tremble.
> I followed God's way.
> Jesus keeps me from the bottom of the pit.
> His love saved me.
> Yahweh light took me from the pit to his running water river
> To drink, then dive deep in his sea of joy.

Gretchen's round face glowed. The pink in her cheeks looked even more healthy as they talked about Willa Dorsey. They had heard her in person for the first time at Swansons'. Mary had looked around the room watching the expressions of the people who listened. It seemed to her that every pore in almost every body in the room was open to the ministry of Willa's music as she sat with eyes closed, playing the piano and singing. The sound of redemptive suffering mingled with childlike joy as she sang, captivating her audience.

"Mom, isn't Willa beautiful? It seems to me that her face shone from the inside out, as if she had a light inside. Her black skin looked almost white to me as she sang."

"I know. I saw that too. Almost a translucence."

"Do you think Dad will go hear her tonight?"

"I hope so." Mary shrugged her shoulders. "I bet he would if he knew you've been fasting for three days so he'd go."

The brown eyes challenged her. Her heavy brows drew together a little as Gretchen said firmly, "Don't tell him, Mom. Promise?"

"I promise, Gretch. I probably won't even see him before we go anyway. I'm not going to wait around for him to come home. That room is going to be too crowded. I want a good seat. If he comes, he comes. It's entirely up to him."

That evening Mary knocked on the door at the top of the stairs in the Swanson home. She held a loaf of bread and a jar of jelly. She heard Willa's voice, sounding muffled behind the heavy door. "Who is it?"

"You don't know me, Willa. I brought you something."

The door opened a crack. The white paint contrasted with her dark skin as Willa peeked out. Mary held out her offering.

"I made this bread today. This is some grape jam I made last summer. I want you to have them. My husband heard one of your tapes, the one about the New York World's Fair. It did something for Norm, to him, I don't know how to explain it. I don't understand it myself, but it was as if you opened a crack in his spirit."

The door opened wider. The purple sleeve fell down in a long graceful fold as Willa held out her hand.

"Why, thank you. I'm glad you told me." Her eyes narrowed a little as she looked intently into Mary's face. "What's your husband's name? I'll pray for him."

"Norman."

"Norman. Norman." Her hand felt warm and firm as Willa patted Mary's arm. "That's a nice name. I like that name. Now you believe God with me for Norman, do you hear?"

Mary blinked back the tears as the door closed. She

hurried down the stairs. The room was filling up, although the meeting wasn't scheduled for another half-hour. Mary saw Scott, Josh, Gretchen, Heidi, and Becca sitting on the floor in front of the piano. Josh held David on his crossed-legged lap. Krista and Becca were leaning on Gretchen. She had an arm around each of them. Mary took a chair halfway down the circle that lined the large room dominated by the shiny blackness of the grand piano. She saw Willa walk down the hall and stand by the door as Jack opened the meeting with prayer. Mary was unaware of the passage of time as Willa sang, until the familiarity in the sound of a nose blowing caught her attention across the circle. Mary looked across the room. She saw her husband. He held his glasses in his hand. He was wiping his eyes. Mary realized that this was the first time she had ever seen him cry.

The phone rang the next day, shortly after Norman left the house. Karen's voice came across the wire, an excited whisper. "I can't talk long, Mary, but pray. Pray hard. Norm is in the kitchen talking to Willa. I'm keeping everybody out. I'll call you when he leaves."

That night Mary sat on her bed, the spiral notebook open and resting against her knees as she wrote.

> God bless Karen for sounding so happy when she called. She called back after Norm left and said they talked for over an hour. She didn't know what they talked about, but she said she had never seen Norm look so happy.
>
> I went to see the doctor today, the OB man who delivered Becca. I have been intending to see him for a long time. It's becoming more and more difficult for me to respond to Norm sexually. The doctor said sex is more in the mind than in the body. He asked me if there were some problems in our marriage. I told him that Scott is getting worse. I started to cry. The doctor's eyes looked very soft and sad.

Scott's emotional control is going. He gets extremely angry. He's becoming less and less interested in his leather work. He never reads any more. His coordination is slipping fast. He can't make his fingers do what he wants them to do. It's very frustrating for him. He really blows up. The girls are acting as if they're afraid of him. The doctor agreed that this doesn't help our sex life. I didn't tell him about Norm's drinking. What would be the use? What could he do? The only way we have ever 100 percent communicated is with our bodies. If this goes, there won't be anything left.

Josh has been awfully quiet lately. He has spent a lot of time in his room, alone. I asked him what has happened to Trish. He just said, "She's gone." Last night he asked me if I had any more typing paper. I asked him if he had been writing, and when he said he has, I asked him if I could see any of what he has written. He handed me a stack of poems. I like them. It may be my prejudiced mother's opinion, but I think they are quite good. One sent tears racing down my face.

Mary reached for the pile of papers on her bedside table, leafed through it until her eyes found the one she wanted.

I'll put it in my pocket, take it with me when I go.
Was my good night kiss that made it so.

What hurt was she didn't know I wasn't there,
    when her sighs were kisses on my chest,
Arching body, closed eyes, longingness of hers to mine,
    caught me cold as windblown snow pelting on a face,
        as clouds left the moon, and shadows swooned.
She put my hand on her breast, held it there, then turning
        ran up the stairs.

I remember once on a windy day how her eyes
matched her face,
    posed lips echoed her grace.
All that she blew and tugged me like the wind in her
hair.
On the ground her locket with a broken chain,
    silver so small in my hand.
I'll put it in my pocket,
    take it with me when I go.

I realize, as I read it again, that the sorrow I feel is my own. My heart did quick flashbacks of her face, those big eyes which slowly opened to trust as we talked. O Lord, take care of her. Speak to her. Protect her. Draw her to yourself. Be to her all hope, all joy, all love.

After she had gotten into bed and turned off the light, she lay awake, her mind skittering about in the darkness. An hour later, she reached over and turned on the light again. She opened the drawer and took out the notebook and pencil. She wrote, crossed out, wrote again.

It was right, that feeling I had when I first set foot on the farm. It is going to be ours. I got a call today from the chairman of the investment fund. They have changed their minds. They want to buy part of it. He said they would arrange the finances to suit our needs. Praise the Lord. Norm doesn't even know yet, he must be out drinking. Somehow, tonight, I don't even care. If God loves us enough to give us that beautiful farm, he will take care of us, no matter how much Norm drinks.

Karen called today. She said we had both been asked to be on the board of Women's Aglow, which is a charismatic women's luncheon group. We have gone to a couple of the meetings; it's just getting going in the Milwaukee area. They are springing up all over the country. I see it as a very good thing.

They don't emphasize any group or church, but just Jesus. I said I would pray about it. I would love to do it. Those women all seem so happy, as if they know a special recipe for joy. But I don't know. Norm is already so threatened by my outside involvements. I'll just have to pray about it. Karen asked me to go to the luncheon Friday.

Sitting at the luncheon table on Friday, Mary watched the women at the head table. She listened as the trio at the microphone led the women in the theme song whose words described the faces she watched: "I'm aglow, I'm aglow, with the Spirit of the Lord." She felt herself caught up with a warmth and joy that was contagious. She listened with interest as Esther Wessling, a woman she had met at Swansons', was introduced as the featured speaker. Esther immediately captured the interest of her audience. As Mary listened, she realized why she had been so impressed when she first met Esther and her husband.

"Let us start with a prayer. I ask, Jesus, that everyone here will look into her own heart and see the need she has brought. We know that you, Jesus, are the one who meets every need. Sometimes, I know, we have to be brought low before we can look up and love. We have to really feel unloved. I ask this day, Jesus, that you will wrap the blanket of your love around each of us this afternoon. Amen.

"I grew up in a so-called Christian home. I think it was. Both my parents knew of the Lord, and really did love him. But somewhere in the process of being reared in the church and attending church, attending Communion, I lost the heart of the message. My head was crammed full of Bible passages and knowledge, but it never made that crucial one-foot jump between my head and my heart. It was many, many years before I knew the difference, but I sensed in my own life that something was missing. There was an emptiness there. I didn't know what it was..." She went on to share her previous alcohol addiction and the freedom she found in Christ.

Mary's heart began to pound as she listened to the story with the familiar ring. Was this why she had felt the mystic sense of destiny when she had first met the attractive woman and her handsome husband? She looked at the tall, slender speaker whose eyes sparkled with life. She had been an alcoholic? This beautiful woman, mother of five healthy children, wife of a minister, intelligent and articulate—alcoholic?

Her mind was oblivious to the conversations in the car on the way home. She was ferreting out the implications of what she had heard. The conclusion was so obvious, she couldn't understand why she had never seen it before.

"Norman is an alcoholic."

Two weeks later, as Mary walked up to the modern brick building, she felt a constriction in her chest. Breathing became difficult. She was glad she had worn the red pant-suit. Red always made her feel brave.

"Hello. My name is Jim. What can I do for you?"

The big man behind the desk had blue eyes that looked at her with intensity. She felt their power.

"I heard a woman speak about alcoholism at a luncheon a couple of weeks ago. I think my husband may be an alcoholic."

"Who was she?"

"Esther Wessling. Her husband is a Lutheran minister."

"Oh yes. Did Esther send you to me?"

"Yes. I went up and talked to her after lunch. She suggested I come and talk with you."

"Did you tell your husband you were coming?"

"No."

"Do you think he would come in and talk with me?"

"I know he wouldn't."

"Then I'll have to work through you. First, I'll go through the stages of alcoholism. Then I'll give you some literature for you to take home and study. If you decide this really is your problem, you can come back and see me again."

When Mary returned in three weeks he looked surprised.

"Mary, I certainly didn't expect to see you again so soon. There is an average span of two years between the first and second visits to this office."

"I don't have two years."

"You have decided, then, that Norman is alcoholic?"

"Yes. The kids and I took that test, the one with twenty-one questions. Gretchen got nine 'yes' answers, Josh twelve, and I answered eight, for sure."

"Most people don't make up their minds this fast."

"Most people don't have a son with a brain tumor. One aggravates the other. I can't handle both. I'll go down the tube."

Mary stopped at Karen's on the way home.

"He told me that if Norm wouldn't come to see him, he'd work through me. He said if I did the right things, and didn't do the wrong things, Norm would quit drinking. He said, 'I can help you have a husband who is nicer than the man you have known.' "

"Do you believe him, Mary?"

"Yes, Karen, I do. It seems completely illogical from all past experience, but he instilled confidence in me. He sounded as if he had promised this many times, and the promise had come true."

"I hope so, Mary. I really like Norm."

"He likes you too, and Jack and the kids."

"I know God has great plans for Norm, Mary. Don't stay away too long on your trip with the kids. Don't leave Norm alone too long. Jack and I want you and your family to stay here until the farm is ready. Please feel welcome to come back any time."

"Thanks, Karen. You don't know how that helps me, knowing we can come home to you all here."

Mary stood up, brushing the grass from her slacks. "I'd better go. I'm making myself a dress for Josh's graduation tomorrow."

"I wish we could see him graduate."

"I do too, but there aren't enough tickets. We're going out for pizza afterwards. I wanted to have a party, but he said no."

The next evening, Mary's feet slapped the steps hard as she ran up the stairs and down the hall to her bedroom. She walked to the door of the closet. She pulled a white shirt from a hanger and laid it on her bed. The sleeve of the navy jacket swung defensively as she yanked it from the closet bar. She laid the blue pants with it on the bed, pulled the red tie from the rack, and threw it on top of the suit. She opened the drawer of her husband's dresser, took out underwear, socks, and a handkerchief. She put them on the bed beside the rest of the clothes. She slammed the drawer shut and walked over to stand at the window that overlooked the road. Her eyes, turning to the clock on the dresser, caught the title of a pamphlet, *A Guide to the Family of the Alcoholic*. She walked over to the dresser, picked it up, and sat down on the bed. As she opened it, her eyes fell on the words, "A wife needs to take a good look at her own involvement with the alcoholic before any steps should be taken to aid in abstinence from alcohol. In most instances, a change in the family is necessary before a change in the alcoholic may be anticipated. To do nothing is impossible. As a general rule, to do nothing means to give in to the situation, to be run over and exploited, and to fight back in quiet, passive, destructive ways."

"OK." She stood up and threw the pamphlet on the bed. "I'll quit being so passive. I'm getting active right now." She ran down the steps. Becca was coming in the front door as she reached the bottom step.

"Come on, Becca." Mary reached for her daughter's hand. "You and I are going to look for your father. He went downtown at eleven this morning to get cigarettes. It's 4:30. We have to be at school at 7:30 tonight for Josh's graduation. I'm going to go crazy if he doesn't come home pretty soon. We'll just go find him."

The little girl thrust her thumb in her mouth as her short legs ran to keep up with her mother's long strides. Mary gave no explanation to her neighbor when she asked to borrow the car. She drove off, gravel flying. She parked in front of the shoe store next to the tavern. She opened the car door for her daughter and held out her hand.

"Come on." The small hand clutched hers tightly as they walked up to the window. The red beer sign blinked off and on. The light blinded Mary's eyes as she scanned the backs lining the bar. Mary felt suddenly dizzy as she recognized the plaid on the broad back of the man sitting halfway down the line of men.

"Come on, Becca. He's in there. We have to go get him."

Stale smells greeted them. Smoke, mixed with the acrid odors of sweat and liquor, mocked their noses as they blinked their eyes in the dark gloom of the long room. Mary ignored the male stares as she walked up to her husband's back. He turned as she stood beside him, his face expressionless. He motioned to the empty stool beside him.

"Sit down, I'll buy you a beer."

Mary swiveled on the ball of her foot. Becca's little legs ran as her mother walked swiftly out of the door. She looked up at her mother, a puzzled frown creasing her forehead as Mary stopped in front of the window of the shoe store, apparently examining the bargains there. Mary breathed deeply for several moments, squeezing her daughter's hand. She turned and walked back into the tavern. Her husband seemed unaware that she stood beside him once more. He drained the glass he held in his hand, then pushed it toward the man behind the bar. The bartender took the glass, pulled down the spigot. He didn't look at the tall woman holding the small girl by the hand as he filled the glass and put it back on the bar in front of his customer. He lifted the bottle of brandy, raising his eyebrows questioningly. Norman nodded his head. The bartender picked up the small glass, filled it, put it down beside the glass of beer.

The question shot out from between her clenched teeth. "Do you realize that Josh graduates tonight?"

Norman picked up the small glass. He held it to his lips. It was empty when he put it back on the bar. He took the glass of beer, drained it, pushed it back to the bartender who was wiping glasses, apparently absorbed in lining them neatly underneath the bar.

"We have to be at school by 7:30. Shall I call a cab so we can get there?"

His eyebrows met as he faced her. "What's all the excitement about? It's only five o'clock. Sit down. Have a beer. You need something to calm you down. You're acting like an idiot."

She shot the words out at him in an angry buckshot barrage. "Supper is in half an hour. We have to be at school by 7:30."

She walked out of the tavern. The short legs ran to keep up with her. Becca stuck her thumb in her mouth as she ran.

They ate supper without him. No words were spoken when Norman opened the door from the garage as Mary was washing dishes, and walked through the kitchen.

The ride to school and the graduation ceremony felt unreal to Mary. She had been so happy, looking forward to Josh's graduation. It had seemed such a victory, the triumph of good over evil.

Sitting in the pizza parlor where they went to celebrate, Mary tried to hide her feelings from her children. She ignored her husband's conciliatory glances. Mary felt alienated from all of them, as the children reacted with giggles to Norm's good mood.

Home again, Norman walked to the refrigerator. He spoke, without looking, to his wife. "Want a beer?"

Mary ignored the question. She followed the children upstairs. She hurried into her nightgown. She crawled in bed with Becca. Cradling the already sleeping girl in her arms, she fell asleep.

CHAPTER NINETEEN

WITH OR WITHOUT NORMAN

Mary walked quickly down the path to the small lake behind the monastery. The sun sparkled on the water as swallows dipped and dived in graceful curves. Mary saw Cy's black-robed figure sitting on the stone bench on the shore. She heard the bells chime in the church tower behind them. The priest heard her approach and stood up, a welcoming smile on his face. He held out his arms. As she walked up to him, he gave her a firm hug, releasing her quickly. Mary felt a surge of comfort.

"Thanks, Cy. You don't know how much I needed that." They sat down on the bench. "I can stay just a minute. I didn't want to leave without saying good-bye, to thank you for all your help."

"Don't sound as if you were going away forever, please, Mary."

She let out her breath in a deep sigh, mingled with a rueful laugh. "Is that the way I sound? Maybe that's my secret wish. I felt kind of guilty when the realtor raved about how nice we are to get out of the house a month before we legally have to. If she only knew how glad I am to be leaving."

"What's Norm going to do while you're gone?"

"Stay with Mom and Dad. We're taking Ebby to a farm near ours. Norm didn't want to put him in a kennel, and Mother can't stand him. She says he's spoiled. I think that bothers Norm more than me going off into the wilderness alone with all the kids—leaving the dog alone."

"How about when you come back? Didn't you tell me on the phone that you can't get into the farm until just before school starts?"

"Yes. We're going to move in with the Swansons. Norm's not too happy about that, but there's not much choice, really. We have to live somewhere. I think it's wonderful of them to take us in."

"It will probably be good for you to get away for a while."

"I can't leave too soon to suit me. I need some time to think."

She looked at the man sitting beside her, suddenly aware of how close she felt to him. She saw the shadows beneath his eyes, the depths of emotion in their deep grey. Impulsively, she put her hand on the black-gowned arm.

"I'm going to miss you, Cy. I don't know how I would have lived through these last few months without you."

The priest smiled at her. "Not me, Mary. Christ." He drew a small New Testament from between the folds of his gown. He leafed through it and began to read. His voice was soft and warm with a familiarity that suggested the book was almost unnecessary. " 'Abide in me, and I in you. As the branch cannot bear fruit of itself, except it abide in the vine; so neither can ye, except ye abide in me.' That's all you have to do, Mary. Abide in Christ. He is the vine. That means you don't have to be. Use his roots. Use his sap, his sustenance, the food he gets from his Father. You don't need to worry about the fruit. He will produce it, through the food he gives you, the branch. He has already given you plenty, do you know that? God loves you very much, Mary, that he has allowed you to suffer as you have, to be continually tested and tried. I don't know what he wants from you, but we don't have to know. Just abide in him. The character of the fruit is always determined by the vine, Mary, not the branch."

Mary sighed. "In other words, quit worrying."

"Yes, quit worrying. I know you can't begin to see any sense in the things that have happened to you and to your family. But God's ways are not man's ways. He is infinite, we are finite. Just rest in his arms. Let him carry you along. 'All things work together for good for those that love the Lord, who are called according to his purpose.' 'Press forward to the mark, to the high calling of Christ Jesus.' Think about these Scriptures, Mary. Christ has called you. He has been calling you for years. He knows why he's calling you. He will complete his work in you, and in Norm, and in the kids. You just have to believe that. Claim the gift of faith. Substitute Christ's faith for your fear. Take the gift he is holding out to you, his faith. Do you realize what that really means? Do you know what Christianity could do if we quit trying to use our faith, and used his instead?"

Mary got up from the bench. "Don't get up, Cy. I have to run." She stood looking down at him, strangely inarticulate. His smile matched the sudden flow of warmth that filled her as he took both of her hands in his and squeezed softly. She turned when he dropped her hands and walked swiftly back down the path to her car.

July 12
Dear Journal,

Here we are at the island. Thank God. I feel as if I can really breathe for the first time in months. The air is so clear. The silence almost shouts, "Be still and know that I am God."

The first day we revisited all the beautiful spots we remembered. The little enchanted pond is still magical. I could almost see Scott's feather angels in front of the canoe. The same beaver spanked his tail at us as he dived under the water. The driftwood is white and shining along the shoreline. The smoke from our campfire drifts slowly upward, the only sign of man we can see. Thank you, Lord, for bringing us safely home. I feel as if this is our haven of refuge.

July 19

I miss my husband's presence as it used to be, when we sat around the campfire together when the kids were all tucked in their tents. We used to drink a cup of tea together before we crawled into our big double bag, never saying much as we watched the fire, never needing to say much. Those nagging, persistent questions come out to taunt me in these moments when I am alone. "What about Norman?" "Who is Norman?" I have to answer honestly, "I don't know." Right now he seems to me a sick caricature of his former self. The steady, dependable, loving man I married is gone.

A crow flies overhead. The harshness of its cry cuts into my thoughts, mocking my questions. I tuck them away in the corner of my mind.

July 20

I'm comforted when I think of returning, with thoughts of the farm. I know God has given us the farm. He must have a reason, or reasons. I don't have to know what they are. It's as if by giving us the farm, he has given me faith. "From faith to faith," as Paul said. One gift, then another. How good God is. How seldom I realize his mercy to me. I know he'll take care of us on the farm, with or without Norman.

I have never before put the thoughts into words: "With or without Norman." After I wrote them, I got up and walked out to the point. I felt all alone in the universe as I looked toward the magic pond.

The tall pines, pointing straight up with stiffened spines, give me courage now. "God," I prayed the words aloud as I stood on the point, "if it means giving up my marriage, I give up my marriage. All I ask is that you save Norman's soul before he dies."

July 22

I think I've passed some kind of milestone. I feel as if I were supposed to be on this particular island at this particular time. I know somehow God is going to put all of this together, in his own time, in his own way. I feel a new sense of purpose, yet undefined. I have a degree of detachment I have never before experienced.

After I snuggled down in my sleeping bag last night, I lay listening to the sounds. The frogs and crickets sang a quiet lullaby. I thank God for the healing of his holy land, for that is what the north is to me. Scott has been very happy here. He has slept a lot. He hasn't participated in what the other kids were doing, but he has been at peace.

CHAPTER TWENTY

AN ULTIMATUM

Mary volunteered to clean up the kitchen after dinner, realizing her mixed motives. She was so grateful to Karen and Jack for taking them in, but sometimes the number of people seemed a bit overwhelming. If she offered to do dishes, she would have some time to herself. She kept glancing at the clock as the minutes turned into hours. Still no sign of her husband, whom she had expected to come in time for dinner. Hiding from her feelings, she busied herself straightening cupboards after the dishes were done and the floor swept. She was relieved when the phone rang and she heard her husband's voice.

"Mare, I've been out looking for Eb, but it got too dark to look any more. I went out to the farm where we left him. Mrs. Wendy said she had called everyone around. Nobody has seen anything of him. He's trying to find his way back to the old house. I'm sure of it. I don't know why it's taking him so long. It's been over three weeks that he's been missing."

"Maybe you should go look around out there."

"I just did. I asked all the old neighbors. They haven't seen him either. I told them to call us if they see him, only I gave them the wrong number. Call all of them and give them Swansons' number, will you? Call anybody you can think of who might recognize Eb."

"Where are you now?"

"The phone booth in front of Red's. I'm just going to have one beer. Then I'll be right there."

"Don't forget, this house gets locked at eleven."

"I said one beer, didn't I? It's only nine now."

Mary hung up the phone. She picked up the receiver and started to call one of the old neighbors whose number she remembered. Before she had completed the last two numbers, she took the receiver from her ear and stood looking at it. She shook her head and hung it up. She spoke aloud in the quiet kitchen.

"Why should I call them, God? If he wants them called, he can do it. He doesn't have to stay down there and drink beer."

Mary sat by the window in the silent house, the Bible on her lap. She had told Jack when he went out to the porch to lock the door that she would stay up to wait for her husband. Jack had nodded his head. She was grateful that he hadn't questioned her. She looked out on the slope of the lawn as the moon shadowed the large pine on the ground in front of the window. She saw the headlights when they cut the dark and circled over the bridge, up the hill toward the house. She walked out on the porch and waited by the door. Norm spoke to her as soon as he stepped on the porch.

"Did you call all the old neighbors?"

"No."

His voice rose. His eyebrows creased together. "Why the hell not?"

"I thought if you were only going to have one beer, you would be home in time to call them."

"I didn't tell you to think. I told you to give a damn about that dog. You really don't care that he's lost, do you? You don't care about a damn thing. Do you know I only had one clean T-shirt today? You can't say you have too much to do around here, with all these people to do the work. Where in hell are all my T-shirts?"

Mary turned her back and started walking away from him. He reached out, grabbed her arm, and pulled her back toward him. "Come back here. I'm not through talking to you."

He took her shoulders in his hands. His fingers pinched into her muscles as he shook her roughly. She clamped her lips tightly together. Hate shot from her eyes and struck sparks from the flinty brown of his.

He pushed her from him. She thudded against the cupboard along the wall that held David's toys. The harsh tom-tom of his words beat out at her, rattling the toys in the cupboard behind her.

"Mary, I've had it. I'm going to the lawyer tomorrow. I want a divorce."

Mary just stood and looked at her husband. It was the first time either one of them had used that word. It seemed to echo off the walls of the porch, ricocheting back at them.

"Divorce, divorce, divorce."

She turned and walked through the door and up the stairs.

The gulls dipped over the lake the next morning when Mary walked down the hill. She sat down on the grass along the shoreline. The water lay quiet, reflecting the clouds and the filtered rays of the sun that hid behind the trees across the lake, sending out long, slender fingers to explore the morning.

Absorbing the peace of the lake, her solitude soaked up the turmoil of the night before with a thirsty sponge, wringing it out over the toes that splashed softly in the water. Her memory carried her back to another lake where she had taken refuge from another angry person, she couldn't remember just who, perhaps her mother?

As the sun rose over the lake in her past, meeting the sun rising over the lake in front of her, she felt the same sense of the everlasting presence, blotting out pain. She sat for long quiet moments, then opened the blue leather book she held in her hand.

Her husband was sitting on the bed when she walked up the stairs into their room an hour later. He held a copy of *Popular Mechanics*. He looked up when she came in the room. He smiled as if nothing had ever come between them.

"Hi, where have you been?"

"Down by the lake reading my Bible. Did you have breakfast?"

"Yes. That Denise can really cook, can't she?"

"She's amazing for her age." She sat down on the bed beside him. "Norm, do you know what I'd like to do today?"

He cocked his head to one side; his tone was guarded.

"No, what?"

"Take a picnic lunch and go out to the river, just the two of us."

"Fine. Let's go. Where are the kids?"

"They're down at the lake. They'll be all right. Karen said she would be home all morning. She'll keep an eye on them."

The sun reflected off the river several hours later as they sat at the picnic table, coffee cups in hand. The smoke that blew off the charcoal grill carried with it the memory of the steak they'd just eaten.

Norm smiled. "I'm glad you suggested coming out here to eat, just the two of us."

Mary did not return his smile. Her face assumed determination as she sat up a little straighter. "I suggested coming out here for a reason, Norm..."

He cut into her sentence as his eyes took up the attack immediately. Hot words matched their glare. "I've seen those pamphlets you've left lying around. I'm not an alcoholic, if that's what you're going to say."

Her shoulders slumped. She felt his words punch out her breath. She was unable to speak.

"I never fool around with other women."

"What's that got to do with it?"

"A lot of other guys do."

Mary looked out at the river. Her eyes followed the swallow that dived down and then swooped up and away, wishing she could hitch a ride on his back.

"I never have blackouts."

She looked across the table at him. Her eyes squinted with the memory of the night before.

"Do you remember telling me last night that you want a divorce?"

"I never said that."

"You have blackouts."

Mary took a deep breath and swallowed hard, willing the tears to stay down.

"Norm, I decided when I was up on the island that I am no longer willing to go on living like this. I have only one life to live. I'm not going to spend the rest of it being miserable. I'm going to be happy. The kids are going to be happy."

She stood up. She walked around in front of her husband, where he sat at the end of the picnic table looking away from her. She didn't speak until he looked up at her. Her voice was sharp, emphatic. His eyes squinted almost shut as he heard her say, "You have to take your choice. It's your family, or it's liquor. You can't have both."

Mary swiveled away from him and walked to the car. She opened the door and slid in. Norman got up from the table. He picked up the coffee cups and put them in the open picnic basket. He closed the cover, walked over to the car, and opened the trunk. He plunked the basket down, slammed the trunk. He got in on the driver's side, turned on the ignition.

The seconds stole into minutes, picking up small bricks of silence as they slipped stealthily by, to build an invisible wall between them as they drove back to Swansons'.

CHAPTER TWENTY-ONE

GOD OF HEALING

Gretchen was feeding Karen's birds the next morning when her mother walked into the dining room. As she put the plastic cup back on the bars of the finch cage, the little birds flew in a chirping flock to perch on the swinging bar above it. Gretchen smiled at her mother.

"Who's leading Bible study this morning, Mom?"

Mary made a face. "I'm afraid I am. Karen asked me a long time ago when she told me she had to be gone today. I wish I'd never said I would. I'm no Bible teacher."

Gretchen laughed. "I've just decided I'm spending my morning on the lake."

Mary finished reading the text with the words, "For that reason those who have wives should stay as free as possible for the Lord; happiness or sadness or wealth should not keep anyone from doing God's work."

She looked around the circle of faces looking expectantly at her. She felt at a complete loss. Desperately she asked the question, "Does anyone have an experience from her own life to illustrate what we have read?"

The only young woman in the group spoke in a voice that was soft and breathy. "I think I do."

Mary looked with grateful interest at the pretty girl with the large, dark eyes and hair that floated a soft cloud around her small, round face.

"When I heard the words, I thought of the first Christmas Peter and I were married." The older women smiled at her. She seemed to warm to their interest.

"Peter is my most precious possession. I love him more than I thought it possible to love anyone before I met him. As soon as I started going with him, I realized I was falling in love with him." She corrected herself with a little shake of her head. "I knew I had already fallen in love with him.

"But when he asked me to marry him, I couldn't say yes, like I wanted, because he wasn't a Christian. I had to pray about it. I did pray about it, and it seemed God said no. But the very next morning after I had decided I couldn't marry him, before I told him my decision, Peter went forward in the chapel in college and accepted Christ. And so we were married.

"And then, on the first Christmas we would have together, he told me he wanted to go to California to spend Christmas with his brother. I said, 'Oh, Peter, our first Christmas,' but as I prayed about it, it seemed all right for him to go. I went home to my mother's, and I had a very nice Christmas. After Peter came back from California, his brother wrote that if Peter hadn't come, he would have killed himself."

She raised her eyebrows, her eyes widening. "What if I had said he couldn't go? So isn't that maybe sort of what Paul was saying with these verses, that Peter was staying as free as possible for the Lord?"

Every head in the circle nodded in agreement.

"And then, the next Christmas, John wrote and asked Peter to come to California again but Peter said, 'No, this year you come and spend Christmas with us.'" Her cheeks dimpled. "And he did."

After the meeting was over, Mary went in search of her new friend. She found her lifting a baby out of the crib in the bedroom at the top of the stairs.

"Thanks, Sharon, for rescuing me. I didn't have the slightest idea what I was going to say." Sharon sat down on one of the twin beds, hugging the blonde baby. She smiled at Mary, who sat down on the other bed. "I think it was your sharing your life with us that started the other women talking. I could hardly shut them up when it was time to close the meeting."

"I notice you used *The Living Bible*. Do you like that paraphrase, Mary?"

"Oh, I love it. It's made the Bible really come alive for me. Are you familiar with it?"

Sharon laughed. "I should be. Peter's dad is the Kenneth Taylor who paraphrased it."

Mary was shocked. "Your father-in-law wrote this?" She held up the green book in her hand.

Sharon nodded. "There are ten children in the Taylor family, and Peter's dad wanted them to read the Bible. But he realized they couldn't understand much of it when he tried discussing it with them. So he just started writing it out in his own words. When he read his version to his children, they understood it and started getting excited about what they heard. So he kept it up when he was commuting to work on the train. He couldn't sell it to anyone, so he quit his job and started putting it together himself, with Peter's mother, right on their own dining room table."

"Wow, that took courage, with ten kids."

Sharon nodded. "Really. They had very little for a long time."

Mary shook her head, remembering Sharon's earlier words. "You know, I never thought that anyone who could do something like paraphrase the Bible would have any trouble with his own children."

Sharon laughed. "Oh, the Taylors are all very human. They're no different from anyone else."

"Have you been here before, Sharon? I don't remember meeting you."

"Just once. I had heard so many strange things about this place that I thought I'd find out for myself. It's not at all as I expected it to be. I feel very good here. It feels just like my home church to me."

"I feel good here too. It isn't like my home church, but

this fellowship has just about saved my life. Our oldest son has a brain tumor—that's what brought me here. I've kept coming, though, because of the love I've found, and the acceptance of my feelings, even my fear."

"I know what you mean. Peter has a bad heart, a very bad heart. I decided when I married him that I could only expect to have him until he is twenty-seven, but I knew I would rather spend a few years married to Peter than a thousand with anyone else."

"What's the matter with his heart?"

"It has a very irregular beat, something to do with one of the valves. He spent a year in the hospital when he was a boy. Sometimes it hardly beats at all, and then it pounds and pounds. I can hear it slushing at night; it sounds like a waterfall."

"Have you ever heard of a man named Harry Greenwood?"

Sharon shook her head.

"Karen says he has a healing ministry. She knows of a lot of people who have been healed by his praying for them. Do you think Peter would come to a meeting while Harry is here? He's coming in a couple of weeks."

"I think he would. He was going to come with me this morning, but the tractor broke down last night. He's working on it right now."

"Do you live on a farm?"

Sharon reached for the green sweater hanging over the top of the playpen and started putting it on the baby. "Yes, we rented the house because it was the cheapest one we could find. Then Peter became interested in planting some corn, so he talked the landlady into renting him some of the land. The old tractor we bought is almost falling apart. He's been working on it ever since we got it, fixing something."

"It's a good thing he knows how."

"He doesn't. He's teaching himself."

"Maybe my husband could help him. He knows everything about cars. I don't imagine a tractor is too different."

Several nights later they all sat around the table in the farmhouse kitchen after Norman had helped with the tractor. Mary, still tired from the move into their new home, silently praised the Lord for this opportunity for relaxation. God had indeed been good to the Soergels.

Norm held the baby on his lap as he talked with Peter about the problems of planting corn. Mary leaned back against the chair, pondering the recurring sense of familiarity she felt, as if a piece of the puzzle of their lives was being put into place by a divine hand. Why should she feel this sense of destiny? She looked at the slim, bearded man talking to her husband. He was young enough to be his son, but Norman spoke with respect to him and listened with interest to what he said. What was it God had in store for all of them?

Several nights later, Mary was standing in her own kitchen, filling the large coffee urn, thinking of all the things she had to do before her guests arrived, when Sharon walked into the kitchen, carrying Preston. Mary raised her eyebrows questioningly.

"Where's Peter?"

Sharon's usually calm voice was ruffled. "He dropped us off. He said he had to go to the feed mill."

"He's coming back, isn't he?"

"I hope so. What time are they coming?"

"It will be at least an hour. Karen called. She said so many people had been at the house all day that they would be late."

Sharon sat down at the kitchen table. "I hope Peter comes back."

"I hope he does too." Mary plugged in the coffeepot. "I hope he likes Harry. Have you asked him if he is going to Swansons' to hear him tomorrow night?"

"No, I'm afraid to ask him. I'm afraid he'll say no."

Mary sighed. "I know how that is."

"I've been praying and praying." Sharon hugged the baby as the line of cars drove in the driveway. Mary caught Sharon's eye a half-hour later as she walked toward the door to greet Peter, who had just driven in. Sharon nodded, letting out her breath in an inaudible sigh of relief.

As they finished dessert and people started drifting away from the dining room table, Mary looked at Sharon. They shared a smile of conspiracy. Peter and Harry sat alone at the dining room table, absorbed with one another. Harry was listening to Peter read from a book he had borrowed several weeks earlier. Mary resisted the temptation to sit down and listen too. She cleared the table without disturbing their conversation.

The sumac that lined Swansons' driveway glowed fire-red as the headlights of Taylors' car shone on it as they drove away from the Friday night meeting.

"Sharon." Peter looked at his wife, holding the sleeping baby on her lap. "My heart was healed tonight."

She smiled at him. "I know."

"Do you know when?"

"When Harry said that there was someone in the room with a bad heart, I knew it was you."

"I thought so too. But when he said that person should come forward, he was looking on the other side of the room."

"I know."

"When he said, 'I'll pray for you anyway—claim your healing,' I remembered what Watchman Nee said in the book I read at Soergels'."

"What did Nee say, Peter?"

"He said, 'God does according to what man is able to take in.' So I did what Harry suggested. I took in my healthy heart."

They told Mary about it several nights later, as they sat

around the table in her kitchen. Peter's eyes shone as he explained what had happened.

"Harry said, 'Don't look for symptoms.' So I lay on my side all night. That way I couldn't hear my heart if it did pound."

Mary looked at him skeptically. "Then you don't really know for sure that your heart is healed, do you?"

"Oh, yes, we do." Peter's smile was triumphant. "Yesterday I was carrying a big box of apples down into the basement. I automatically stopped to rest at the bottom of the stairs, like I've always had to do to wait for my heart to quit pounding. Only yesterday, it didn't pound. It was beating normally. I wasn't even short of breath."

Sharon smiled at the memory, "You should have seen his face when he came running up the stairs to tell me. Last night he slept flat on his back, and we didn't hear a single heartbeat."

Peter handed Mary the paperback book he carried. "Here's Watchman Nee back, Mary. Thanks for letting me read him. I think he's the one who really convinced me healing is for me."

"Read it to me, Peter, will you? I think I need to be convinced too."

He opened the book. "I opened right up to this page when I picked it up in your living room one day. 'Be it therefore apprehended that the spiritual blessing we receive in sickness is far inferior to what we receive in restoration. If we rest on God for healing, then naturally after being cured, we will continue to walk in holiness so as to preserve our health. By making us well, the Lord possesses our body. Unspeakable is the joy found in a new relationship and a new experience with him, not because of sickness cured, but because of a new touch with life. In such a time, believers glorify the Lord far more than in the time of ill health.' "

They sat quietly for a moment. Mary's eyes held a memory when she looked from Sharon to Peter.

"You know, I think I experienced the sensation people describe when the Holy Spirit becomes real to them when I was in the Isolation Hospital in Milwaukee when I was twenty years old. My body was almost completely paralyzed. I was in terrible pain, but about four o'clock every afternoon when I heard a church bell, I felt the most beautiful sense of peace, a deep feeling of joy—I have never felt like that since. There aren't even words to describe how I felt. It has made a difference in all the days of my life since that time."

Peter smiled at her. "I know what you mean, Mary. That's how I feel these afternoons when I'm up in the apple trees picking apples. I sing in the Spirit." Peter reached for the *Living Bible* lying on the table. He opened it with familiar fingers. His voice was strong as he read to them.

"Even the wilderness and desert will rejoice in those days; the desert will blossom with flowers. Yes, there will be an abundance of flowers and singing and joy! The deserts will become as green as the Lebanon mountains, as lovely as Mount Carmel's pastures and Sharon's meadows; for the Lord will display his glory there, the excellency of our God."

As he looked up from the green Bible, Mary pointed out the window. A cardinal was perched on the lowest branch of the oak tree by the driveway. Bright red feathers were outlined against the blue of the sky as it raised its head in a burst of song.

CHAPTER TWENTY-TWO

BESIDE STILLWATERS

The rays of the sun shot across the horizon as Scott and his mother walked down the lane between the stream and the alfalfa field. Heifers grazed on the hill ahead of them, black and white polka dots against the green.

"Look at that, Mother. Isn't that a picture? See the cow on the top of the hill, silhouetted against the sky."

"Yes, Scott. Aren't you glad the pastures were rented for grazing when we moved here? It makes me feel like a real farmer."

"It's still hard to believe, isn't it, that this is actually our farm?"

"It is, Scott. Every time I come around the bend in the road before the bridge, I catch my breath to believe it really is true."

They walked in silence under the willow trees, stooping to escape the low branches as the stream narrowed the path that led to the spring, and then went on up to the top of "Picnic Hill." Mary hopped ahead of Scott over the large stones that formed a natural bridge across the stream where the water widened.

"Let's sit down a minute, Mother." Scott's voice was a little breathless. "I want to tell you something."

The ashes within the circle of stones blew up in a small grey cloud as Ebbie plopped down at their feet. The friendly pet had returned to the friends who were caring for him when he ran away—after Karen and Norm had prayed urgently about the matter.

213

Scott leaned back against the thorn apple tree. Mary picked up the pointed stick, with the memory of burned marshmallows sticking to the end, and began poking at the fire, long dead.

"You know, Mom, last Saturday when I went down and asked Father Bob to pray for me because I was having such a terrible time controlling my temper, do you know what happened?"

When he paused for a long silent moment, Mary looked at her son. He was watching the clouds in the sky blowing high above them. His eyes were luminous as he looked back at his mother.

"Father Bob said his anointing oil was still in his bag in the car, it was so early in the morning. He had to go out to get it. When he left the room, I started to pray in tongues, and you know what, Mother?"

"No, what, Scott?"

"You know the head of Christ he has over the mantel in his office, the one with the sort of wispy hair?"

Mary nodded.

"Mother," his voice fell almost to a whisper as if he relived the experience he was describing, "that picture turned into the whole figure of Christ. There was an angel on each side of Jesus, and they didn't leave when Father Bob came back in. You know, Mother, I had four people praying for me, not just one!"

The wind blew softly against their faces. The rustling of leaves as it touched the tree above them was the only sound as they sat together.

"Do you know what Sharon told me yesterday, Scott? She said they had a letter from Peter's father in answer to Peter's letter describing the healing of his heart. At the very hour that Harry Greenwood was praying for Peter's heart, Dr. Taylor was flying over India reading the Bible. He had been praying for a healing of a relationship with one of his children. When he came to a passage where Jesus healed—I can't remember for sure, I think it was a

Roman officer's servant—but there were words that Jesus spoke, something like 'Go home, and what you believe will be done for you.' Dr. Taylor claimed those words for the healing of his son. He marked the time down on the margin of his Bible. Scott...'' Mary's voice sank almost to a whisper, "it was the very same hour Peter's heart was healed.''

"There really is healing power in God's Word, isn't there, Mother? Remember the night you read me the Twenty-third Psalm, the night before I went to the hospital in Milwaukee?''

His mother nodded.

"I was thinking about that after Father Bob and the angels prayed for me. It's really true, the Twenty-third Psalm. God really is our shepherd, Mother.'' He smiled at her. He patted the ground beside him. "He has even given us some of his pastures.''

"Scott, that's it!'' Mary's voice was quick with excitement.

Scott's eyebrows arched the question, "What's it?''

"You've just named the farm!''

"I have?''

"Yes, you have. We'll call it Stillwaters.''

"Mom, that's perfect.'' He pointed to the pond far from them, at the very tip of the farm. The water lay quiet, mirroring the blue sky puffed with clouds.

"He leadeth me beside the still waters.''

Mary scuffed her feet through the leaves as she walked down the slope past the silo. She climbed over the fence, stood undecided for a moment, wondering if she should go towards the high hill or back by the pond. She looked away from the hill, turned instead to the path that led by the stream which was low now, as if the water were weary of rushing, just waiting for a rest under the coming blanket of snow. A few brown leaves clung stubbornly to the oak that marked the beginning of the trail the cows had

cut through the steep bank on the back of the farm, hiding
the pond as she walked toward it. Only the diving swallows betrayed the still blue jewel, reflecting the late October sky. Set in a ring of grass dried to a golden hue by
the sun, the water lay quiet, as if to absorb as much of the
warming rays as it could before it lay paralyzed, its surface
that chose to dance to the summer imprisoned by its own
cold chill.

Mary kicked the apples away from the tree halfway up
the slope, behind the church. She smelled their protest as
they rolled away from her. She sat down under the tree,
leaned her head back, closed her eyes. She felt the sun,
warm on her face. When the dog flopped down at her feet,
she opened her eyes. She reached in her sweater pocket,
took out her notebook, and began to write.

> Dear Journal,
> I don't know what's the matter with me. The sun
> feels so bright. I feel so dull.

Her left hand felt in the pocket of her sweater.

> I found a poem Becca wrote the other day when she
> was mad at Norm.

She unfolded the square of paper. The letters were so
small she had to squint to read them.

> I'm just a piece of dust waiting for someone to find,
> and when they do, I hope that I can trust him,
> for he's broken too many promises already, just too
> many.
> When will I be found? When will the sun shine
> again?
> My tears are just the rain.
> The rain is up in the clouds, but I'm waiting to be
> found
> And promises made again and promises made again
> and promises made again.

I know how she feels. I feel like a piece of dust too. I think I have been keeping my feelings on ice for so long, now that Norm has quit drinking and I don't have to be afraid any longer, I don't know what to do because the ice is melting. Maybe that is how Becca is feeling. I've been writing lots of poetry too.

She leafed through the notebook, read over the last poem she had written.

> Love was a duet of purpose,
>   a cell of creation,
>   union with God,
>   response to his master plan.
> Love was a green garden gate
>   freshly painted
>   blown open on a warm spring day.
> Love was an old glove,
>   softly worn,
>   caressing each finger in easy familiarity.
> Love was the sudden explosion of sunset after a
>   summer storm,
>   kaleidoscope of color,
>   blending into sleepy dark.
> Now the gate is scarred by kicking booted feet.
> The torn glove falls into crushed garden flowers.
> My sky's a dull slate grey, streaked with pain.
> Must I, Lord?

I wrote that the other night after I saw Jim, at Lutheran Social Services. Norm went to bed early. I just didn't feel like going to bed, so I stayed up and wrote.

I went to see Jim because I really shocked myself last week. Norm was fixing the tractor and went downtown to get a part. He didn't come back and he didn't come back and he didn't come back. I was sure he was drinking. When he did come home, his eyes were clear and bright, not dull and foggy. I shocked myself. I was mad at him because he hadn't been drinking. I had worked myself up into a rage and I didn't know what to do with it. Jim said I shouldn't worry about it. He said it took us many years to get where we are today, it's going to take time to get our lives, and our feelings, rearranged. He said this is what is meant by alcoholism being a family disease. I told him about Becca's apparent hostility toward her father. He said that this is part of the disease too. He said I should go to Alanon, get the kids to Alateen if they will go. He said people who have felt, and still feel, like we do can help us the most. I asked him if he thought Norm had quit for good. He said, "How can I know that? I'm not God. But look at it this way—if your husband had leukemia and had a remission, what would you do? Would you enjoy his health while it was good, or would you spend all your time wondering when the disease would recur?"

I've been reading over some of the poems I've written since Norm quit drinking. I don't like what I see.

Mary leafed back through the journal, her eyes stopping along the way.

Life's patterns interfered,
Funnel clouds blown across the sky touch down,
     suck up,
Greedy with a thirst that will return.
Quiet ponds blown wild,
Deep whipping whirlpools pull persistently.
Legs kick frantically,
As hands reach toward heaven.

She turned the page, read lines that had been crossed out, rewritten, then scratched over with an impatient pencil.

The cat hides behind a mouse mask.

Mildew stains the cover of his fencing manual, for-
  gotten on the bookshelf
Beside the Boy Scout handbook.
The cat uses a mirror for his shield,
Sheathes sharp swords in soft pads of words dis-
  guised as fun,
Pounce, release, then catch again,
Clawing scabbed layers of remembered
  vulnerability.
Absorbed with his mirrored image, he does not see
  his paws drip red.
I run away, hide in white sheets,
Closed eyes my shield against the trap I'd labeled
  "love."

I'm sure the feelings evidenced in those lines are
what sent me in to see Jim. They must be the reason I
was sorry Norm was not drinking. I think, down
underneath, maybe I wanted an excuse not to go on
trying any longer. I decided it is time I quit hiding
the way I feel on white paper, and get it out into the
open with a counselor I trust, like Jim.

I felt for awhile that it would be disloyal to God to
go for professional help for myself. I realize now this
was spiritual pride, and false judgment on my part.
Who am I to say that I am too spiritual to need special
help? I am a weak human being just like everybody
else. I am a sinner. I hate, I resent, I fear, like anybody else. I don't have to preserve an image of om-
nipotence. God can take care of his image, I don't
need one. All I need is to be, to become.

I know now why I was afraid to walk up the steps
to the Lutheran Social Services. I was afraid of my
own feelings.

Lord God, help me to be honest with myself, and
with you. Help me not to be afraid to expose my bad
feelings. I believe in the resurrection of the body,
help me to believe in the resurrection of a marriage.

CHAPTER TWENTY-THREE

REBIRTH

Mary wrote in her journal one April evening.

> I wonder if real authors are like me, writing when they are unhappy, frustrated, scared, worried; not writing when they are happy? Is that why so many writers lead such tumultuous lives? Does creativity breed turmoil, or does turbulence foster creativity?
>
> But that's not what I want to write about. I want to write about living. About being born, if you are a sheep, or even if you are two sheep, one white, one black. And I want to write about being reborn, if you are a marriage, and you are almost twenty-one years old, for that's what has been happening at Stillwaters. What happened this morning proved it to me. For the first time, Norm and I worked together without any major argument.

It had all started when Norm went off to work in the morning. He told Mary, "Be sure you keep checking on the sheep. Ruby looks about ready to pop."

Mary checked Ruby in the morning. She checked Ruby in the afternoon. She checked Ruby before she went to bed. She came in from the barn about ten o'clock. She took out the notepaper for shopping lists and sat down at the kitchen table, pencil in hand.

"Norm, you'd better check Ruby when you get home. Her rear end looks pretty pink to me. Wake me if you need me."

She didn't hear her husband come to the bedroom. She was sound asleep. But she woke up fast when she felt his hand pushing up and down on her back, none too gently.

"Wake up, Mary. Wake up. The lamb's head is out. I don't know what to do."

Her head felt groggy. "What time is it?"

"I don't know. About 4:30. Come on, get up."

She jumped out of bed, pulled on slacks and a sweater. As they ran through the yard, the broken windows of the chicken house where Norm had housed his sheep welcomed them with a gap-toothed grin, reflecting the full moon that hung low in the sky. Norm's longer legs carried him in first. Mary looked across the partition that separated the chickens from the sheep, to where he knelt, beside the fat body, dim in the darkness of the shed.

The partition was chin high. Mary asked him with a puzzled frown, "How did you get over there?"

"I crawled over. There," he pointed. "Put your foot on this piece that sticks out. Jump down when you get to the top."

"I can't do that. I'd break my neck."

"Then you'll just have to go out and open the gate in the yard and crawl through the opening the sheep use."

As Mary crawled through the hole low in the wall, her hands on suspiciously smelling moist ground, she wondered just whose bright idea it was to get sheep in the first place. She stood up in the shed. It was almost too dark to discern the fuzzy round body that stood with her back to her, apparently oblivious to the fact that there was a small head protruding from her rear.

"Why, the head is perfectly dry." She gasped. "It must have been sticking out for hours."

She felt a surge of sympathy for Ruby, having such a difficult time expulsing the lamb. She could empathize with that situation. What she could not understand was her attitude of apparent unconcern. Mary put her hands on the side of the little head. The eyes stared unblinkingly at the buttons on her sweater. Mary gave a little tug. Not even an eyelash moved. She looked down the back of the sheep to her husband. He was kneeling by Ruby's head, murmuring in soothing tones. They shrugged their shoulders, a duet of helplessness.

"All I can remember is Nita saying, 'Sheep are terribly dumb. You have to help them lamb.' Why didn't we ask her, 'Help them how?' "

"Go call her up."

"But Norm, it's not even five o'clock yet."

"Well, do something. Pull on the head."

"No." Mary shuddered at the picture that suggestion evoked. In her mind's eye she saw the neck getting longer and longer, an elastic band of wet pink wool. "I'll go call Nita."

Her friend's voice sounded more shocked than sleepy when Mary apologetically explained the situation.

"That's awful. We once had to cut a lamb's head off to save the mother. Is the head swollen?"

"I don't know. I didn't see it when it first came out."

"You have to push it back in."

"You have to what?" It was Mary's turn to sound shocked.

"You have to push it back into the mother."

"The head?"

"Of course the head." Nita sounded cross. "The feet have to come out first. You have to push the head in, then go in with your hands, get hold of the feet, and pull them out. Let's see, how can I explain it to you?"

Mary sat down on the radiator cover. Her legs felt weak.

"First, you have to make sure that the chin doesn't catch on the pelvic bone and go up and back. Then the lamb would never come out. Put your right hand into the cervix. Feel for the shape of the head, find the forehead. Put the palm of your hand on the nose and push down. But gently, very, very gently. But first you have to put your left hand in and find the front feet. You pull them out slowly as you push down on the head. Have you got that?"

"I hope so." Mary repeated the instructions.

"Good luck. Call me back. I want to know what happens."

Mary ran down to the shed, carrying a pan of hot water, remembering the way her hands had felt as she had wiped them on her slacks. She handed the pan over the partition, ran out into the yard, and made a quick reentry into the delivery room.

Norm listened to what Nita had said, his eyebrows touching, his forehead wrinkled.

"You'll have to do it. My hands are too big."

Mary looked at his hands. She put hers by his. She nodded her head in reluctant agreement.

Mary washed her hands in the warm soapsuds. She put them on the sides of the little head. She gave a weak push. She dropped her hands to her side. She shook her head at her husband and shrugged helplessly.

"I can't, I just can't do it. I feel like I'm drowning the poor little thing."

"You can do it, Mare. You can do it." It was the same tone that he used with the sheep.

"Mother, what are you doing?" Gretchen's face peered across the partition. "Oh, is she having her baby? Wait for us. I'm going to go wake the other kids." They heard her feet pound out.

"Here, Mare." Norm straddled the sheep, facing his wife. He leaned over, putting his hands under the sheep's belly, supporting her. "I'll hold her up like this. Now you push the head in. Come on. Push."

Mary closed her eyes. She put her right hand on the lamb's forehead, which felt like a soft warm blanket. She felt the slight bones beneath her fingers.

Mary moaned as if to say, "You're going to have to do this. I can't. You know I can't."

She put the fingers of her left hand into the moist passageway, opening it with spreading fingers as she pushed against the bones under her right hand. The eyes remained open as they disappeared.

"You're getting it. You're getting it. That's the way." Norm's voice rose excitedly.

"Oh, God," her voice rose almost to a shout as the canal closed with a slurp, "don't let the poor thing die in there."

Her right hand followed the little head, scraping past sharply tightened bones into the warm cavern full of slimy curves and knobby angles.

"Please, God, help me," she whispered. "I don't know what a leg feels like. Oh, here's a knee, I think."

She pushed her fingers down the little leg.

"Here's a hoof, Oh, Lord, don't let me break this leg." She squeezed the hard little triangle between her index and third fingers, straightening it slowly. She wedged her left hand in beside her right wrist. Ruby resisted the invasion. She edged into the back of Mary's wrist as her voice rose rebelliously.

"That's all right, girl, it's all right." Norm spoke softly. "You'll be just fine."

"Let's see." She tried to remember. "Nita said to get the foot out but keep the chin from going back." Her left hand felt along the leg she held firmly in her right hand, slid down the curve of the little shoulder.

"This leg feels like it's pointing straight back. How am I ever going to turn it around?" Mary's fingers slid down the leg. Ruby squeezed against Mary's arm. Mary hooked four fingers behind the small stick-like leg, pulled it slowly forward. She grabbed the hoof with her thumb and index finger. She heard chattering voices as the little hoof tried to escape. She opened her eyes to see four pairs of eyes lined up like headlights over the top of the partition.

"One of you, get over here. I need somebody to hold a foot." Gretchen scrambled across the top.

"Here, Josh." Norm spoke up. "You come and hold the lantern for your mother, so she can see what she's doing."

Mary spoke quietly to her daughter.

"Squat down, Gretch. Try not to get in my way. Take this little hoof. Josh, shine the beam right here." The little triangle gleamed like a shining black diamond. "Don't let go, Gretch. I'm going in with my right hand again and try to get the head lined up."

She pushed her hand over the top of the two small legs, slid it up the pointed chin, over to the hump of the forehead. She curved her fingers over the head as she pushed gently down with the heel of her hand on the nose. As the nose went down, she wedged the small head between her index and third fingers, pulling gently. She straightened the left leg and eased it out under the head.

"Here, Gretch. Take this other little hoof and pull slowly as I pull on the head. Norm, push on the belly."

She shook her head as he pushed his hands together.

"No, not like that. Push back, like you were her belly muscles trying to push the lamb out."

He pushed down and back.

"That's better." She nodded her head. "OK, now I'll count. When I get to three, Norm, you push, and we'll both pull. One, two, three."

The slippery body slid quickly out. The tight white curls were coated with an orangy wax-like substance. The body lay motionless. Ruby ignored the apparently lifeless shape that lay beside her on the hay. She panted with deep, shuddering breaths.

"Easy, girl, easy." Norm looked down at the still form as he squatted by Ruby, rubbing her head behind her ears.

"It's dead, isn't it?"

Josh lay down in the hay, blowing softly at the small mouth where the tip of a pink tongue protruded. He picked up a wisp of hay and held it in front of the nose.

"No, Dad. It isn't dead. Look, it's breathing."

As if blown by a very tiny breeze, the hay moved almost imperceptibly.

"Maybe you should pick it up, Mare. Give it artificial respiration."

"No, I don't think so." Mary's voice carried real authority. Her maternal instinct took over. "I think we should leave it alone. Ruby should know what to do, I should think. She isn't doing anything, so I don't think we should either."

As if she understood the words, Ruby turned her back on them all. She walked over to the corner, where she stood motionless, head down.

"Mary!" Norm's voice rose in excitement. "Look, there's another one coming out."

"No. That must be just the afterbirth." She looked at the mass bulging from the rear that faced them. It was shiny black.

"No, Mother. It's a lamb. Look, you can see one hoof."

"Oh, no. Not again." Mary groaned as a small black head slid out, then stopped moving.

"It's a black sheep. It's a black sheep." Josh's voice was exultant. "Peter and I have been wanting a black sheep. I told him we would have one first."

"You're going to have to push this one back in too, aren't you, Mary?" Sympathy tinged Norm's tones.

"I'm afraid so. Nita said both feet have to come before the head. At least this one isn't all dried out."

This time she felt much more sure of herself. She delivered the small body in record time.

The slim front legs bent as the black lamb struggled to get to its feet.

"Look, it wants to get up already."

"He sure came out easier, didn't he, Mother?"

"Do you think the white one is all right? It hasn't moved." The quartet of voices babbled excitedly.

"I think so. It seems to be breathing more deeply. It probably will just take a little longer to pep up, I suppose, the birth was so difficult."

As the small black nose nuzzled her side, Ruby turned

towards her baby. Her voice rumbled deeply as she nuzzled the lamb, sniffing over the entire body. Next she explored the small still form that lay on the hay, her nose softly curious.

"You kids better go get ready for school. You're going to miss the bus." Norm seemed to suddenly realize his own family responsibilities. "Come on up, Mary. Let's have a cup of coffee."

"No, Norm. You go. I'm going to stay down here for a minute." She realized that her legs suddenly felt weak. She sat down on the hay, leaned back against the wall.

Gretchen turned to look back at her mother as she neared the door. "What are we going to name them, Mom?"

"Let's name the white one Miracle." Heidi spoke across the partition. "It's a miracle she's alive."

"How about naming the black one Preston?" Josh spoke up eagerly. "Maybe Peter won't have a black sheep of his own, but at least there'll be one named after his son."

The laughing voices faded away. She listened to Ruby rumble at her lambs with a voice she had never heard her use, low and intimate. She heard the roosters signal to the sun, which shot golden rays through the cracks in the shed. She smelled the fresh hay Norm had used to make a clean bed for Ruby before he went up to put on the coffee-pot.

"A manger's not such a bad place to be born, after all." She knew her whisper would be heard, and understood.

"You're just in time to hear Willa." Norm put the coffee cup down in front of her as she walked in the kitchen door and sat down at the table. "I just put on one of her records."

They smiled at each other across the table as Willa started to sing the words that were in their hearts.

"He's the greatest shepherd of all."

CHAPTER TWENTY-FOUR

THE CHRISTIAN RAILROADER

As the group finished singing a song of praise, Karen stood up, fastening the microphone around her neck as she started to speak.

"Next Sunday we are going to start another 'Life in the Spirit Seminar' at five o'clock, if any of you would like to sign up. This is the eighth of these series we have taught here at Living Waters." She picked up a small white booklet from the top of the pile on the piano. "This is the book everyone who takes this course uses. Look through it if you like. This seminar is taught by Jack and me and our three spiritual advisors, Father Dick Korzinek, a Catholic priest; Rev. Ferd Bahr, a Lutheran pastor, and the man we all call 'Dad' Ziemann, who is an Assembly of God minister who lives here on the grounds and shares in all the ministry. If you would like to be a part of this study, please sign on this list." She picked up the clipboard lying on top of the piano. "I think that's all the announcements I have."

Jack stood up as Karen sat down. "Tonight we are going to be hearing the testimonies of another of our core group families. The core group meets at seven o'clock on Thursday nights. Anyone who would like to be a part of this service group, which has formed since we have grown so large, is welcome. Tonight we are very happy to be hearing from the Norman Soergel family." He looked over to Norm and Mary who sat with all their family in the front row. "Who's going to start—you, Norm?"

Norman picked up the *Living Bible* that lay on his lap. He stood up and walked to the front of the group. He waved away the microphone Jack offered to him. "I don't need that thing, thanks." He opened the Bible to a little scrap of paper. The rustling in the room stopped when he started to read.

" 'Several days later he returned to Capernaum, and the news of his arrival spread quickly through the city. Soon the house where he was staying was so packed with visitors that there wasn't room for a single person more, not even outside the door. And he preached the Word to them. Four men arrived, carrying a paralyzed man on a stretcher. They couldn't get to Jesus through the crowd, so they dug through the clay roof above his head and lowered the sick man on his stretcher, right down in front of Jesus.

" 'When Jesus saw how strongly they believed that he would help, Jesus said to the sick man, "Son, your sins are forgiven!" But some the Jewish religious leaders said to themselves as they sat there, "What? This is blasphemy! Does he think he is God? For only God can forgive sins."

" 'Jesus could read their minds and said to them at once, "Why does this bother you? I, the Messiah, have the authority on earth to forgive sins. But talk is cheap— anybody could say that. So I'll prove it to you by healing this man." Then turning to the paralyzed man, he commanded, "Pick up your stretcher and go on home, for you are healed!" ' "

As Mary listened to her husband, she heard his feelings in his voice. She realized the group behind her could feel it too, they were so still. She marveled at the grace of God, and thanked him for the wise, godly counsel they had both received from Jim at Lutheran Social Services. Norm had long ago given Christ his heart, but when he was finally able to also give God his will, he found freedom from the slavery which had been destroying him for so long.

As Jim had said, the first step for the alcoholic is to admit he is powerless over alcohol. Even believers in Christ can be alcoholics—Norm was proof of that. But thank God—the long battle had finally ended in victory in Christ. Mary remembered that Norm never actually said he would quit drinking—he just did! Praise God!

Norm put his finger in the Bible to mark the place. He got right to the point.

"Mary and I went to the Christian Railroad Convention in Toronto, Canada, last week. It's the second year we have gone. On the way home, I told her I wanted to talk to you all, to thank you for praying for me through the years. If it hadn't been for your prayers, I wouldn't be passing out these *Christian Railroaders* to the guys I work with." He took the small newspaper out of his shirt pocket and held it out toward the crowd. "I'd have been going down to the gin mill after work to drink with them. I told my wife God must have been driving that car for me hundreds of nights when I drove those forty miles after hours of drinking."

Norm raised his hands, as if holding on an imaginary steering wheel. "You know, when I was trying to quit, I really had to fight with my car." He twisted the wheel. "It wanted to turn into the tavern so bad and then, somebody would say a prayer, and that car would straighten right up and drive on home."

He pointed to a lady in the front row. Mary flinched inwardly, remembering the impact of that accusing finger. "You're smiling. You think you were sound asleep, not praying. Maybe you said a prayer that morning, and God used it when he needed it. You don't think God is limited by our timetables, do you? Sometimes the car would win, and I'd go as far as the parking lot and sit there shaking, I wanted a drink so bad. I'd really have to pray. But God answered my prayers. He answered your prayers. I haven't had a drink for eighteen months.

"He healed me of smoking too. Of course, I had to go to the hospital with a bleeding ulcer first, but when I was there, Karen and Margaret came to see me. Margaret's left now, but she could really pray. We went into the chapel and Margaret put her hands on my head and prayed. When I got back to my room, I took off my moccasins and looked at the bottom of my feet. My wife said, 'What are you doing?' I said, 'I'm looking for the hole in my foot. When Margaret prayed that I would be healed from the top of my head to the soles of my feet, I felt something go out of the bottom of my feet.' " He stopped until the laughter subsided. "You know something? I haven't had a cigarette since. I still want one, but I haven't smoked any."

Norman opened the Bible again and began to read. " 'They couldn't get to Jesus through the crowd, so they dug through the clay roof above his head, and lowered the sick man on his stretcher, right down in front of Jesus.'

"What do you see when you hear that? What if Jesus were in this room, right now, healing people? Would you have the guts to climb up on the roof with a friend and start pounding a hole right there?" He pointed above his head. All eyes turned to the ceiling. "Can't you see the plaster fly around? That beautiful light fixture—do you suppose that would fall down, breaking into a thousand pieces? I wonder what the people beneath them thought?" Norm turned to Jack. "I wonder what the owner of the house thought?"

Jack's booming laugh led the others.

Norm waited for the laughter to stop. His tone softened. "Do you know who can have that kind of faith today, the faith to pound holes in roofs, and pray for healing? We can. You can." He pointed around the room, then put his finger on his chest. "I can." He pointed at his wife. "I am sure glad she did. I'll let Mary talk to you now."

Mary took the microphone Jack handed to her. "That's really a miracle, isn't it?" Her dimples echoed Karen's as she looked across at her friend. "Karen could tell you just what kind of a miracle it is, but it isn't because of my faith." She pointed out the window at the lake. "That lake is about ten inches higher than it would have been if I hadn't cried so much sitting in this room. It was other people's prayers that were answered, not mine, because I didn't for one minute think Norm would quit drinking. The only thing I did was keep coming, keep praying, asking others to pray." Mary paused a minute, gathering her thoughts.

"You know, alcoholism is really a family disease, but it is an illness that doesn't show on the outside. It's an illness we all hide. We are ashamed of it, until we really come to understand that it is a disease. It isn't good or bad, or right or wrong; it's sick or well. It's nobody's fault, any more than any other disease is somebody's fault. Sure, the alcoholic has made some wrong choices, but so have those who are ill with high blood pressure, diabetes, heart trouble, and most other illnesses. We don't blame them because they're sick, we don't blame their wives. So don't put the blame on alcoholics, or their families. That's part of their disease, the attitude of most people they know. That's why they hide it so long, until they can't any longer. By that time they're usually all too sick to help themselves.

"Did any of you who stuff that empty hole in yourself with food when life isn't going right ever stop to think that that is exactly what the alcoholic does with liquor? You know, we got a letter today from Norman's mother. She told us about the retirement party the city of Yuma, Arizona, had for his brother Ed, who was forced to give up coaching because of the terrible hereditary disease Huntington's disease, which kills slowly and horribly over a period of fifteen years. Ed is such a great man that five of his teachers flew out from Eastern Illinois State University to pay him tribute. One of his coaches said he threw a ball farther than he has seen any man throw. I doubt that he could throw a ball three feet today. How do you think you would feel if you were a boy growing up with a father dying of that disease? My husband was such a boy. How would you feel if you knew half your father's family was dying of the same disease? If you discovered something that could temporarily erase that kind of fear from your mind, do you think you might just be tempted to use it?

"Did you know there are eighteen million alcoholics in this country; that is, diagnosed alcoholics? How many are still in hiding? Did you know that each of these sick people affect at least six other people? Did you know one out of every eight people who drink is alcoholic? Don't you think it is time those of us who say we love the Lord try to learn a little about this disease, so we can help people get well? I think it's time we started pounding holes in their ceilings too."

Mary looked at Karen again. "That's what these people did for me, they helped me get well. They have helped my family get well. So have a lot of other people. You know, alcoholics are really more fortunate than most sick people. There is something they can do to get well. Quit drinking. And what other disease has a list of people who have recovered from it, who are willing to be called any hour of the day or night like those in AA or Alanon? You know, I feel very angry when I hear anyone say AA or Alanon is not spiritual enough. Alanon is one of the most loving groups with which I have been involved. Sure, they use different words, but they are willing to be vulnerable with each other, completely honest and open. How many churches can say that? You know, I dream of the day when we can combine what we have experienced in the power of prayer, and the know-how of the professional alcoholic workers in AA and Alanon.

"God is really wonderful. He always seems to send into our discussion groups on Wednesday mornings just the people who need to be with us. Since I have talked openly about our disease, alcoholism, three other women have realized their husbands are alcoholics, gone for help, and now have sober husbands, just in the eighteen months since Norm has stopped. Isn't that marvelous?" Mary smiled and shook her head.

"But I'd better get off my soapbox. I could talk about this all night. When Norm said he wanted us to share, I got out a poem I wrote. I wrote this at the end of a long struggle, when I was just beginning to realize my own involvement in the disease, alcoholism. I wrote it after my daughter Gretchen got married. My reaction to her marriage was one that really surprised me. Here she was marrying a wonderful man, one who had graduated from college, had a job teaching, who is a very committed Christian. They had a dream life planned; they are sharing a beautiful farm with Sharon and Peter Taylor, who used to be part of this prayer group. Gretchen met David through Sharon and Peter. Peter had first met David when he went to David's dad's farm to buy some goats. He bought lots of goats, so when David planned to marry Gretchen and found a teaching job only twenty miles from Peter's farm, Peter asked David to farm with him. David knows so much about goats—he is one of about sixty judges of dairy goats in the whole country. You would think any mother would be happy about such a secure life for her daughter, but when Gretch told me she wanted to get married, I was sad. I wasn't just sad, I was absolutely miserable. That's one of the things we do, we who are married to alcoholics. We make our children our parents. I felt like a little girl whose mother is leaving her. Gretchen had always understood, she always knew how I felt. She didn't have to say anything, she would just smile, and I knew she understood. I didn't want to give that up. I spent one whole day out on the back of our farm, walking the hills, wailing. So then the next week, after God had dealt with those feelings, I went back out on the hills and wrote this poem. I'd like to share it with you tonight:

Accept and relinquish—
O Lord God, today, these words seem to stick to my

mind as I pray.
Accept and relinquish, tenaciously cling,
two stubborn bells that continue to ring,
as I walk through the days,
my heart strangely light
my spirit at peace,
my joy clear and bright.
"Accept and relinquish," I hear the Lord say.
"Accept and relinquish, just give me each day.
Please hold out your hands,
wide open and free.
I'll take them, I'll lead you,
please give them to me.
Accept and relinquish, and you'll dwell with me,
Eternally happy,
Abundantly free."

"I think Josh has something to share with you tonight too. Josh?"

When he got up from his chair, Josh looked very tall. His black hair was neatly trimmed. His shirt was tucked in his light blue trousers. He reached in his shirt pocket and took out a piece of paper, and began to read:

Praise the Lord.
He is the carpenter
of all foundations that stand.
He has taken my shaky life,
Not braced it, but built it anew.
Thank you, Lord,
For your strong hands.
Hands of light, of love
That knew nails
and were still
for our sake
that we not be forgotten.

The room was very quiet when he sat down.

CHAPTER TWENTY-FIVE

CROSS OF GOLD

Alone in the house, Mary felt a quick stab of the old pain. She walked to the window in her daughter Gretchen's living room, at beautiful Breezy Hill. The apple trees were puffed with pink. Demurely, they waited on the slopes, satisfied just to be beautiful, content to pay for the privilege of living on the highest hill in the area with the pink and white promise on their branches.

Mary's spirit lifted. It could not resist spring's celebration. Hearing a shout of laughter, she looked toward the barns. Gretchen and David were running out of the milk house. Sharon and Peter followed, Peter's arm around his wife's waist. Tall Josh stooped low as he came through the door so that Preston, who rode on his shoulders, wouldn't hit his head. Mary saw Heidi chasing Becca; they both were laughing. Mary held her breath as she saw Scott stumble as he walked through the door, but his father caught him before he fell. As she watched Norman help Scott walk slowly up the hill toward the house, she marveled at the change in her husband.

Mary recalled the scene in their living room at home the day before, when she and Scott had come home from the appointment with the neurosurgeon. Scott had asked his mother and father to sit down and talk with him. Norman had sat down on his favorite chair in the corner of the room. Scott had gotten up, moved the small wooden chair from in front of the piano close to the couch.

"No, Dad, sit here. I need you close to me."

Scott had paused for a long moment after he sat down on the couch beside his mother, his eyes closed. Mary had wondered if he were praying, his stillness had seemed so intense. When he opened his eyes, she saw the tears. They lay in luminous pools just beneath the surface.

"Dad, yesterday the doctor said my time is running out. I asked him if I would live three more months, and he said I would. He wouldn't guarantee me any more time than that, although he did say he thought I would probably live longer than three months."

His tongue moved with concentration, as if it had to think for itself how to articulate the words Scott thought. His parents watched him closely, concentrating on his efforts to speak clearly.

"Dad, you have Thursdays and Fridays off now, right?"

Norm nodded his head.

"I would like to do all the things we can while I still know what I am doing, all right? I would like to walk in the Kettle Morraine Forest and see the sun breaking through the pines once more. I want to go up to Breezy Hill and stand on top of the big rock where the Indians used to grind their corn, and look for wild flowers, see if there are mushrooms poking their heads through the ground. Someday maybe we could go out in the canoe and float down the river. I remember the exciting feeling going around a bend, wondering what you will find, if a great blue heron might fly off, his long legs like two bent sticks. I asked the doctor if we could go on a trip. He said not to get very far away, but maybe we could camp somewhere for just one or two nights, and I could smell the wood smoke of a campfire just one more time."

He looked over at his mother. Tears coursed down her cheeks.

"Dad, I don't want this to be a burden on Mom, and I don't want it to be a burden on you either. Maybe we'd better just give it to the Lord."

In her memory Mary felt her husband's hand, as he had

reached for hers. She had taken Scott's cold hand in hers, noting the contrast with his father's warm one. She tried to recall the words her husband had said as he had lowered his head, closing his eyes.

"Dear Lord, thank you for Scott. Thank you for Mary. Thank you that you take all our burdens from us. Please help us in the days ahead."

She pictured Norm as he had opened his Bible. He had looked up at Scott, his brown eyes tender, tears brimming but not spilling over as he said, "I want to read you the rule of the day, Scott. You know on the railroad, the safety department always has a rule of the day."

He patted the Bible with his index finger.

"I have a new rule book. I found these words in here this morning."

Norm took out the folded leaflet from the American Bible Society that marked the place and began to read.

"How beautiful upon the mountains are the feet of those who bring the happy news of peace and salvation, the news that the God of Israel reigns. The watchmen shout and sing with joy, for right before their eyes they see the Lord God bring his people home again. Let the ruins of Jerusalem break into joyous song, for the Lord has comforted his people; he has redeemed Jerusalem."

Mary sat on the rock wall on the crest of the farm. It was the fourth year she had watched spring slip under the cover of snow on the hills rolling out before her, to renew her vows with summer. Now the tops of the hills were frosting with a soft green, shading into tones of grey with just a subtle suspicion of the vibrancy that was to come as they sloped away from the sun that was climbing up toward noon.

Mary held a piece of paper Scott had given her. When she had told him she was going out for a walk, he had gone down to his room to get it. Mary wondered again how Scott always knew when she was troubled. He seemed to have some sort of radar beacon tuned in to her emotions and her thoughts. They shared them without exchanging words. When she unfolded the paper, she saw that it was dated "May 23, 1975." Scott had written, "9:00 AM or so. I took a long, soaking bath, and it was so relaxing that I could think above and beyond my human flesh. I would, of course, be aware of my flesh in a small way. Flesh and body were separated by Holy Spirit.

"I thought of the initial semi-shock when Jules D. Levin told me that I had but three to twelve months of life (earthly) left. As I write this now I smile, and with the Lord's radiance about me, praise him.

"Soon after seeing the doctor, one week or so ago, Mom prayed with me. As I prayed, I was given the vision of a cross over my head. It wasn't large, only one or two inches, but I know that the Lord put it there as a reminder that he is always with me, especially to help me and to lift me over earthly trials and tribulations.

"As the days go by, the cross grows larger and more iridescent in a holy way. It is a combination of the purest white and gold and a simple but awesome magnitude.

"Just vomited out (literally) some nasty stuff.

"As I was bathing, I had a mental picture of myself like this" [he had drawn a radiating cross with a small figure kneeling below it], "kneeling in thanks and gratitude for his loving hand over me. Praise Him. Praise Him more and more and more."

Mary reached in the pocket of her sweater and pulled out her notebook. She extracted the pencil from the spiral cylinder and began to write.

Scott's symptoms are getting worse. He is having trouble with balance, he has to hold on to the wall, a chair, anything he can reach to help him walk. He is stuttering, as if his tongue refuses to obey his brain. He told me the other day he is having "mini-convulsions" in the night. He said, "I feel as if I am pinned to the bed. I know what is happening, but I can't move." I have found dried blood on his pillow about five different mornings. I can't tell where it is coming from. There is never any trace of it on his face, or his ears. I don't want to mention it to him, in case he hasn't noticed it. I just change the pillowcase.

Thank God this time Norm sees what is happening. He will talk about it with me. He is being really nice to Scott. He takes him along when he has to go downtown, just like he used to do when Scott was a little boy.

As the sun moved westward, Mary continued to write. She scratched out lines, tore out pages. Her eyes searched the skies, as if the words she wanted were hiding behind the soft white clouds blowing high above her. Finally she was satisfied with the poem that had taken shape as she sat at the top of the hill, a compilation of the fragments that had wisped through her sleepless nights.

> An enigmatic bell I hear; it tolls to me both faint and clear,
> From past to future, yet unknown, my grief plays out its song alone.
>
> The pain I feel cries out to me, "Reach out, reach out, reach out, be free."
> From bubbling brook and leafing tree, I hear its poignant melody.
>
> My praise to you, my Lord, my King, with every cell my life I bring,
> Love's offering on your altar lay, my only wish is to obey.
>
> My God, I give, with open hands, if thy sovereign will demands
> My child, my son, this life most dear to which my flesh would now adhere.
>
> With every note the songbirds sing, promise of new life in spring,

Greening buds on bush and tree, frozen streams,
  now broken free.
I hear thy love, I feel thy peace, thy warm breeze
  brings me new release.
New growth on fields and hills I see, O Lord, you
  plant new life in me.
This pain of nails and thorns and loss you bore for
  me upon the cross.
You took on all this suffering, that I to you my son
  could bring,
With full assurance, God above, that you receive him
  with all love.
Your peace, your hope, your joy I know. A blessed
  circle you bestow,
Transcending our humanity, you lead us to infinity.

Scott was coming up from his room in the basement as
Mary walked through the back door. He looked at his
mother, his eyes bright.

"I was just down in my room, Mom, praying. I was
thinking how lonely Jesus must have been. Just think, all
he had was the cross. He didn't have any Bible to read, to
tell him what would happen after he was crucified. He had
to live it out so we could read about it. I never really
understood how terrible that must have been for him before this, Mother."

Scott held out his hand. "Look, Mom. The puffiness is
almost gone. It started to go away when Dad Ziemann
prayed for me last week. My face is better too, isn't it?"

Mary looked closely at Scott. His eyes looked larger.
They had been almost hidden by the swelling in his face.

"Yes, Scott, it is much, much better."

"I haven't had a headache since the core group prayed
for me last Thursday, and the cross grew so much brighter. Do you know what I think, Mom?"

"No. What do you think, Scott?"

"I think every time someone prays for me, that gives me
one more day to live."

The rooster woke her just as light was sifting into the room. Mary pulled on her robe and walked down into the kitchen. She plugged in the coffeepot. She sat down at the table to look out at the stream until the coffee perked. Noticing that Scott's notebook was open on the table, she picked it up. He had written:

> Monday—May 26, 1975   12:40 PM
> (Memorial Day)
> Beautiful mild day, partly cloudy, nice breeze. Just came up from the stream. ATTENTION MOM AND DAD: I wish that on the day I join our Lord that a fruit tree be planted on the farm. The tree will bear fruit, and those fruits can remind you of my spirit through our Lord that will always be with you. PRAISE HIM! PRAISE HIM!
>
> Have plans to fish in back of the garage.
>
> I'm just so happy because of the Lord's presence always with me.
>
> Last night at Swansons' Sunday night meeting, as I prayed I was shown a picture in my brain like this. [Scott had sketched a head with a circle inside which said "brain area." Inside the "brain area" there was another circle which said "tumor area, white and empty."]
>
> May 26, 1975   12:55
>
> Just received remembrance smile from Andy Ullrich from heaven—nice to know!!!

Mary's thoughts were startled. She had been thinking of Andy so often. It had been such a shock to everybody when the young, talented pianist had died suddenly of a bowel obstruction.

Scott mentioned Andy often in the next several months. His mother recorded it in her journal as she wrote one night, when the house was dark, all but the lamp beside her bed.

Dear Journal,

Scott mentioned Andy again today. It seems to be a real comfort to him to think of Andy in heaven. He has had a good summer. He seems to have had such fun spending the big retroactive SSI check that finally came through. He said, "Mom, I've been asking God to let me live long enough to get it. I want to buy everybody a real nice present." He surely has. He got Gretchen and David the best crib Sears had in the store. Gretchen is bloomingly, beautifully pregnant. She has acted as if it really agrees with her. I can't wait to be a Gram. Scott got me a great big rocker because "every Grandma should have a rocker." He bought the family a set of World Book Encyclopedias, and Gretchen's baby of the future a Childcraft set. Everybody talks about a boy, but I know she is going to be a girl. I think it will be very nice to have a granddaughter. Scott bought Norm a calculator to help him keep his books, Becca a tropical fish aquarium, because she has always wanted one, he said.

Scott seems to be slowly winding down, like a clock that does not have too much more time in it, even if the alarming symptoms have miraculously disappeared.

Heidi is registered for Berea in the fall. Josh has been accepted also, but he is undecided. He is a full-fledged mason now, has done well in the art classes he has been taking at the University of Wisconsin, Milwaukee. Becca is becoming more a farm girl daily. She milks five to six gallons a day.

I feel as if we are living in limbo. Norm and I seem to be, for the first time, in the same place in acceptance of Scott's illness, in limbo. Sometimes I feel as if we are in the calm in the center of the storm, but then I think of what Jim told me, "Would you enjoy the remission if Norm had leukemia, or would you think about when he was going to get sick again?" A chronic illness that is degenerative is like alcoholism, it seems to me. "A day at a time" works best. Growth group at church has taken the pressure off the family a great deal this summer. Scott shared with them last spring what Dr. Levin had said, so they didn't break up for the summer, but kept meeting weekly for his sake. It has helped so much for him to have a group with whom he can be totally honest. The family camping people at church have been wonderful too. A different family has taken Scott each weekend they have camped. It has been so good for all of us.

Mary wrote again one night when the first snowflakes were falling.

It has been a sad fall. Scott has been slowly sinking. Not like last spring, when the symptoms were so scary, but a slow fading away of his physical body, while his spiritual self has grown stronger. He seems to have an inner stillness, a calm, a quiet, a peace. He looks younger. His face often glows, as if there was a light behind it. He talks about the cross above his head more often now. He uses words like "while there is still time," "while I'm aware," "while I still have the energy." If I ask him "why?" he answers, "Because of the way my head feels." He has wanted to spend as much time as he could just being in Oconomowoc, talking to anyone that will talk to him. It is like he is trying to stuff as much as he can into every day. Norman and I have been strangely peaceful about it, even if it is a risk. He goes over to Owen's if he is tired, or takes a nap at church. He takes his sleeping bag to growth group on Tuesday nights and sleeps on the floor of the lounge so he won't miss Wednesday morning breakfast.

Mother died October 15 after a long paralyzed three years in the nursing home. I feel as if she died the day she had her stroke. That wasn't my mother lying there with the tube in her nose, and the frantic look in her eyes. I think it completely cruel to keep anyone alive in that state.

We had to put Gram Soergel in the hospital September 6. I just realized how sad it is that I said it has been a sad fall. Peggy Joanne Considine was born September 8. David and Gretchen brought her down to see Gram at the hospital when she was only five days old, because we thought Gram might be dying. Gram has a nonfunctional esophagus. She has refused a tube. She adores Peggy. She calls her "Little Dumpling." It is quite a picture to see Gram, getting thinner and thinner, holding Peggy with the chubby pink cheeks and the big blue eyes. I held Peggy at Mother's funeral. It was a comfort. We all supported Gram's decision not to be tube fed. She is being fed IV, but she is talking about having that stopped. She talked to me quite a bit this summer about how hard it was for her to see Ed in the nursing home with the tube in his nose. I don't blame her a bit for choosing not to live like that, for with her love of life, it wouldn't be really living. I told our kids when Mother had her stroke and they chose to do surgery to keep her alive, "Don't do that to me. Let me go." I'm with Gram all the way.

She is so brave, all the nurses love her. Several have told me she is the best patient they ever had. She hasn't changed at all, she is still always thinking of the other person, never herself. She always says to me, "Mary, I wish I could be more spiritual, like you are." I told her the other day, it isn't the words we say. Only a saint could die as she is, with such selflessness. What a beautiful example she is setting for her grandchildren. Craig and Wayne come up from Illinois every weekend, they love her so. The nurses always say, "My, you have a devoted family," and she smiles so smugly. Our kids are being so good to her too. The boys keep her supplied with flowers, weekly corsages, and they all go to see her almost every day.

Gayle called the other night. She said the doctor wanted to do a tracheotomy on Edwin "to give him four to six more months of life" and she refused. I think she wanted reassurance that had been the right decision. She certainly got it from me. She sounded so shaky. God help her.

CHAPTER TWENTY-SIX

THE BEGINNING OF BUTTERFLY WINGS

Mary wrote again as the snow blew against the north window. The garden was layered with weeks of falling snow.

Only three weeks until Christmas. I certainly don't feel like celebrating birth. All fall I felt as if there were a big snowball named "Death" picking us all up and carrying us along with it. Incredibly, Gram slowly shriveled away to less than sixty pounds. She died, one little bone-bag of courage. Three days later, Gayle called at seven in the morning. She said they had just moved Ed from the nursing home to the hospital so they could remove his brain as soon as he was declared legally dead. He had chosen to be a donor to the brain bank for research for the Committee to Combat Huntington's Disease. Thank God Gram went first.

Scott is much weaker. He came up from the basement the other day with a glow on his face. He said, "Mom, I had a bad headache, and I asked Jesus to heal me. He said, 'I have healed you, Scott. I am going to complete your healing in heaven.' "

We seem to be living on two different levels. Consciously everybody seems the same. Scott and I can talk about the situation quite rationally. The other day, in a restaurant, we made out a list of people he wanted to get extra Christmas presents for, and a list of what he wanted to leave to whom when he dies. I felt really quite cold-blooded about it. I wondered if anyone could hear us, and what they thought if they could.

But then there are the nightmares. Heidi came downstairs the other day, first thing in the morning, and asked me, "Mother, do you think Scott is going to die?" I nodded my head. She said, "I do too, now. I had a dream last night. I dreamed Scott and I were in a car. We came to a wide river. Scott jumped out and went running over to the edge of the bridge, to take a picture. I got out and stood on the platform that was built out over the water. The river was running very fast, there were big boulders and rapids. As I looked down at the water, I had the distinct impression that Scott was going to fall off." Her voice filled with tears as she added, "And then I wondered if anyone is ever as brave as they seem."

I have been having the recurring dream of racing down a steep hill and my brakes fail, and then I dreamed something worse. I was in a car, but all alone, and I came up to the water. I stopped the car and got out and walked down to the shoreline. I couldn't see across the big body of water. There was an island not far from shore, and Scott was standing on the island in front of a big cave, or tunnel, that didn't seem to have a bottom, at least I couldn't see one. He was calling out loudly in a frightened voice, "Mother, Mother." He didn't seem to see me, so I yelled as loud as I could, "I'm coming, Scott." I started wading out to him. The water was cold; whirlpools tugged at my legs. He didn't see me, for he kept calling, "Mother, Mother," and when I woke up, I could still hear his voice, I could still see him falling backwards into that cave, his body twisting sideways as his legs disappeared from sight. I felt cold all night.

Scott is dreaming too. One morning he said, "Last night I dreamed I was inside an oil tank. It exploded."

Karen and Jack have asked us to spend Christmas Eve with them. This will be the fourth year we have had Christmas together. She has asked her Aunt Erika and Uncle Bud and their ten children. Karen has told me so much about this couple, how they have established a foundation to promote Christianity all over the world, while they live so simply themselves. I am looking forward to meeting them.

Mary felt as if the snow wove a curtain of white, falling slowly on the last act of the play as they drove towards Swansons', Scott between his parents on the front seat of the car. The rest of the family had piled into David's car. As they drove slowly through the swirling snow, Mary thought of the Christmas Eve ten years earlier when it had been snowing so hard. She remembered the ride home from St. Luke's after they had left Scott, and how frightened she had been. She saw, in her memory, the hospital corridor. She heard the voices of the cast of *Brigadoon.* She recalled how Scott's eyes had remained closed as they walked past his door singing of the city that lived for only one day. Mary looked at Scott, sleeping again, but this time with his head on his father's shoulder. She felt a strange sense of peace. The snow seemed to weave the three of them in a snug white cocoon. She sensed the beginning of butterfly wings.

Scott held both their arms for balance as he walked slowly up the walk to the house. The bright Tiffany lamp in the foyer framed a rectangle of blue on the floor of the porch. The smell of wood smoke greeted them as Jack held the door open.

The butterfly burst its prison as soon as Mary stepped into the room, brightly decorated for Christmas. The evening took on an intensity of awareness. She felt as if she were living in a different dimension; as if all the Christmas Eves she had known as a child, all the ones she might never see were part of this particular evening. The people she was introduced to became immediate friends. She knew them intimately.

Her sensory antennae lengthened, multiplied. The sounds she heard coming from the music room drew her like a melodic magnet. The man who sat at the keyboard of the Steinway grand emanated vibrancy. The collar circling his neck looked very white against his dark skin. His sparkling eyes were as black as the clerical suit he wore. His voice matched his music in emotion, as he explained that he was playing his own composition, depicting the bombing of New York City, to portray our apocalyptic time.

Listening, Mary felt as if she were living out the music she heard. As his left hand played out the destruction and anguish, the right hand took up in the treble the peace and joy and beauty that was the spirit of her son. Mary felt as if what was happening in Scott's head was happening to her body, catalyzed by the sounds she heard. Stranger still, the musician-composer seemed to sense her experience. His eyes were knowing as he looked across the table at her as they ate dinner in front of the fire. "Yes," he said, as if the statement needed no explanation, "yes, the Muses recognize one another."

But then, they all seemed to understand her. Aunt Erika and Uncle Bud and their children seemed to know all about Scott, although they had just met him. They seemed to understand how his family felt. They didn't ignore the fact that Scott was different, they marveled at it. Tim, their oldest son, and Robin, the young man from England who lived with Swansons, ate dinner at a small table with Scott. Mary was aware of their unobtrusive assistance to Scott as she listened to the man across from her describe the road that had led from the podium of the Rome Symphony Orchestra to a seminary in Connecticut. It was a fascinating story, the journey from conductor, composer recording artist to Brother Alphonso, who had taken the vow of poverty.

Scott was touchingly childlike in his enjoyment of Santa Claus as Tim donned the red suit for the benefit of the younger children. Santa sat with his arm around Scott as they listened to Uncle Bud read an amen to the evening with the Christmas story from *The Living Bible*.

"Scott, would you like us to pray for you?" Karen asked the question as Uncle Bud closed the Bible. Jack set the chair in the middle of the circle as the families gathered around Scott. They put their hands on his shoulders.

Scott raised his hands in the air, palms upward. His eyes were closed, his head back as his lips formed the syllables of his prayer language. He seemed unaware of their presence, as if they no longer were a part of his reality. His face was luminous.

Norm looked across the circle of faces to his wife. He shook his head. He took out his bandana and blew his nose hard.

CHAPTER TWENTY-SEVEN

THE CURTAIN FALLS

"Dear Lord, clear Scott's mind."

Mary remembered the words of Karen's Christmas Eve prayer as the last notes of Handel's *Messiah* left the air Christmas afternoon and a man's voice started to read a poem she did not recognize. Scott opened his eyes. She thought he had been asleep, unaware of the gloom in the words coming from the radio. Scott's mouth quirked up in a half-smile as he said, his throat dry and scratchy, "Sounds like Edgar Allan Poe, doesn't it, Mother?"

As she nodded her head, his eyes closed once more. He slept until evening.

Mary watched Norm and Josh as they almost had to carry Scott back to the couch when he tried to walk from the bathroom. She followed her husband into the kitchen.

"I think I'm going to stay down here with Scott tonight, Norm, OK?"

Norm nodded. Understanding etched his eyes. "All right, Mare, whatever you think best."

The red and gold balls on the Christmas tree in the corner of the living room reflected the moonlight that poured through the north window as the figures of Mary and Joseph and Baby Jesus slowly stopped rotating. Mary looked at Scott, who had asked her to wind up his favorite gift, "Just one more time, please, Mother." He lay on the couch. His eyes were closed.

As the music box ran down with the strains that matched the words, "Sleep in heavenly peace," Mary remembered the night they had found out about Scott's brain tumor. She recalled the way they had sat around the dinner table and sung "Silent Night." Her memory pictured the small boy walking up the stairs alone, the dog at his heels. She looked at Ebbie as he slept by the couch. The hair on his face was almost entirely grey. She thought of the lessons she had learned about living, and about dying, as her own hair had silvered. She knew now that the ultimate demands of death have to be faced alone. In the death of her son, she was experiencing a part of her own death, the end of a familiarity, the beginning of an unknown. Strangely though, she felt none of the fears the nightmares had brought with them, at this particular point in time when dreams had turned to reality. Mary felt instead wrenched, tugged, torn, divided, separated.

She had been experiencing, in a current that carried itself along in the deepest part of her being, a running dialogue with the Bible. Phrases she had memorized as a child played themselves over and over in her spirit, as if someone had pushed in a tape deck that continued to run on and on. "For the joy that is set before me, I endure the cross." "Let this mind be in you that is also in Christ Jesus." "For there is forgiveness in me." Sometimes they mixed themselves up, sometimes they replayed the same words. They never were silent. They were always there.

She looked at the rocking chair Scott had bought her, silhouetted against the moonlight. It seemed symbolic of the other level she was living. She remembered how she had rocked Scott when she nursed him. She had felt, for the first time, as if she were a real part of creation. Picturing herself as a tree, and the earth that nourished it the form of God, she knew the sap running through her to her baby was the food God had created for him. She remembered the poem she had written as she rocked, with the small body nuzzled to her, feeling his warm breath moist on her breast.

I longed to write or paint or sing,
To do some great, creative thing.
My hands could not tell what my heart had to say,
And then, My baby smiled today!

She wiped her cheeks with her hand. She felt as if the tree were being yanked from the ground, to lie with roots exposed among the litter of Christmas wrappings, impotent, torn, useless.

Mary looked out the open drapes toward the north, thinking how many nights she had sat in the big red chair, as the leaves dropped from the trees and the snow came to cover them, struggling with her feelings as she attempted to write them out. As she tried to remember the lines she had written, Scott stirred.

Mary put her hand on his arm. Scott turned his head slowly. His mother saw that his eyes gleamed with fever. The whites were etched with a web of fine red lines. She leaned closer when he opened his mouth to speak. His voice was just above a whisper, hoarse and dry.

"Mom, I have to leave here now."

Mary swallowed. Her eyelids fluttered. Her bottom teeth caught her top lip, controlling it. She recognized Scott's expression. It was the way he always looked at her when he was concerned about the way she felt. She heard the rattle in his throat as his hot fingers closed on the hand she had slipped into his when he opened his eyes.

"I'll be careful. I'll be careful." His eyelids closed, even before he finished the last word.

Mary sat by the couch, memorizing her son's face. With his eyes closed, he looked so healthy. The fever had painted his cheeks a vibrant pink, a striking contrast to his white skin, so strangely childlike for his twenty-four years. His complexion was soft and smooth, without a hint of beard. His hair was dark against the pillow, matching the eyebrows with the expectant arch that always lifted slightly when a smile lit his face, as it had so often in the past months. Mary remembered what he had said whenever she had asked him if his head hurt, "It doesn't matter, Mother." His face pictured peace. The brow was so smooth, the circles under his eyes were erased. Only his breathing, the heat she felt as she smoothed back his hair, betrayed the deception of his appearance.

As she felt Scott's breath lighten, he opened his eyes again. His voice was both weaker, and more urgent.

"I heard it again, Mother. I really have to go."

Mary breathed deeply. She slipped her hand from his. She patted his arm. "I know. It's all right to go."

His eyebrows raised a little.

"I'd better get my jacket."

Mary's voice deepened. "No, Scott. You won't need your jacket."

"Well, I'd better get it anyway." The voice drifted off.

Tears slid from between her lids as Mary closed her eyes, leaning her head on Scott's chest. Her mind turned itself off. Scott slept on, apparently unaware of the widening puddles on his nightshirt, until he roused again and breathed so softly that she could scarcely hear, "I heard it again, Mother. I really do have to go now."

Mary sat up a little straighter. Her voice was slightly stronger. "I know, Scott. That's Jesus calling you. I want you to go with him."

Scott raised his right knee. It leaned against the back of the couch, then, as if the effort were too much, slumped back down. Scott looked down the length of his body to his legs. When he turned his head toward his mother, she recognized the glimmer of a new idea in his eyes. He raised his eyebrows, as he said with a question mark in his voice, "Do you have an extra crutch?"

Mary leaned her forehead on his arm to hide her tears. She heard him gasp, then cough deep in his throat. She jumped up, ran into the bedroom where Josh was lying. The bed was rumpled, his eyes were wide open. Mary had the feeling he had not been sleeping.

"I think he's going."

Josh jumped out of bed. He walked tall in front of his mother to kneel beside the head of the couch. The moon lit the scene. Josh put his hand on his brother's head. Mary heard an unknown language pour from his lips as he lifted his face, raising his left hand in the air. Mary sat down beside the couch. Tears poured down her cheeks as she clamped her lips together.

Mary did not know how long it was before she heard her husband's steps on the stairs, but the living room was bright with sunlight. Norm took in the situation with a glance. With the sound of his voice, her mind cleared.

"Mary, I think we had better call Dr. Crawford."

She stood up. "I just remembered something. I have to go down to Scott's room. I'll be right back." He heard her feet rushing down the steps.

She was breathing hard when she ran up to her husband, who stood looking out the dining room window toward the barn. She handed him the piece of white paper. She stood close to him as they read what Scott had written in large blue letters. He had dated it April 29, 1970.

"To whom it may concern: I hereby announce that if the time comes and I leave life here on earth and die, hopefully to enter heaven, I will give any and all parts of my body to be used in any way medicine sees fit in order to help another human to stay alive. My heart will do a lot more good supporting another human rather than rot away. Sincerely, Scott Soergel."

Norm looked at his wife without speaking. His face was pale.

"I think we had better call Ben Schumann, Norm. That will have to be taken care of in this hospital. Scott has been carrying a kidney foundation card around in his wallet too."

Josh stepped between his mother and father. He seemed to take on parental authority as he said to his father, "I'll call Dr. Schumann, Dad. Then I'll call Dr. Crawford."

Mary was only dimly aware that the other children were in the room as they waited for the doctor to come. She heard their hushed voices, felt as if they were shadows of a different dimension, living in another world.

Josh picked up the phone after the doctor had come, examined Scott quickly, then left, saying he would meet them at the hospital.

After he had talked with Dr. Crawford, Josh turned to his mother, talking in a quiet, even tone as if to a small child.

"Mom, I'll go in the ambulance with Scott. You stay with Dad. Come with him to the hospital after Dad gets dressed."

The rattle of Scott's breathing was the only sound in the room as they all listened for the crunch of the wheels on the driveway. When the two men rolled the stretcher through the dining room door and lined it up beside the couch, Mary paced with long steps between the living and dining rooms. Her arms were stiff at her sides, her fists clenched. She breathed the words from deep in her chest, repeating the phrase over and over as tears poured down her cheeks, "Oh, God. Oh, God."

Norm sat crumpled in the red chair in the corner. As the stretcher passed through the door, he put his hands over his face. Sobs groaned from deep in his chest. Mary knelt in front of his chair. She reached up, gently pulled at the fingers that covered his eyes. She felt the hard palms as she opened his hands, laying them flat on his knees. She put her face down on his hands. They quieted one another.

As she and Norm drove to the hospital, Mary's mind clung to the words she was sure she heard Scott whisper as the stretcher passed through the door, "I'll be OK, Mother."

When she walked into the Intensive Care Unit, she realized it was all over. The blips were getting slower and slower on the machine on the wall, but that was not what convinced her. When she saw her son's face, she knew from the color that there was no life left. The rosy pink had turned mottled grey.

The doctor turned from the phone on the desk. "Too late, Mary, too late. There's no time to save the kidneys." He turned to the nurses who stood by Scott's side, one checking the IV flowing in his arm, the other with a stethoscope on his chest.

"No heroic measures," the doctor said quietly.

She and Norm nodded their heads, a duet of agreement.

Norm walked from the room. Mary stood with her hand on Scott's chest until the nurses removed the stethoscope for the last time.

CHAPTER TWENTY-EIGHT

LET THE BELLS RING

The phone was ringing. Mary slipped from the bed quietly, trying not to wake her husband. She pulled on her robe as she walked to the phone in the hall. She was surprised to hear Brother Alphonso's voice. He had called last night to tell her, "You had an angel on earth, now you have a saint in heaven." This morning he didn't even say "hello." Instead, rather reproachfully, "Didn't you hear the phone ring earlier?" When she said she had not, he went on, "Last night I was reading my breviary, I should say, this morning. It was about three o'clock; I seldom sleep all night. As I read, I smelled the most delicious fragrance, and I thought immediately of Scott. Then I wrote this poem. I want to read it to you:

O Lord, how can we enjoy the coming bloom of
    spring,
The twittering and chirping of birds on the wing,
Or watch clear brooks splashing mossy stones,
A life that glows in resplendent, verdant tones?
Dear Son, how can we enjoy what's fresh and new,
Mourning each day the loss of you—
Buried on a cold, grey melancholy day,
When the winter winds whisked our love away?
O Lord,
With resignation we'll bear the pain when we see
    Scott's empty room,
Hold back the tears, dispel the nights filled with
    gloom,

259

Because we know down deep, that Jesus took him by
    the hand,
For his reward in heaven—to the promised land,
Beyond the opalescence of infinity,
To dwell with you, O Lord, until Eternity!"

He paused, waiting for her reaction. Mary could not talk. Tears ran down her cheeks. She swallowed twice, then managed a whispered, "That's beautiful."

"You're not supposed to cry. I wrote that to comfort you."

She smiled at the reproachful note in his voice, "I know."

"I just want to say one more thing. Do you remember when you were leaving, Christmas Eve, and I was sitting on the bench on the porch with Scott, who had gone out there to cool off?"

"Yes, I remember."

"Do you know what he said to me? I asked him to pray for me. I told him I was just starting to learn to be a priest, and that it was hard for me. He said, 'I'll be seeing Jesus in just a few days. I'll talk to him about you.' He was looking right at me. I said, 'Are you serious?' He said, 'Sure I am. I'll talk to Jesus about you.' "

Mary wiped her eyes as she hung up the phone. She walked down to the kitchen and plugged in the coffeepot. She heard steps on the stairs.

"Hi, Heidi, you're up early."

"I thought I heard you on the phone."

"You did. It was Brother Alphonso. He wrote a poem about Scott. He wanted to read it to me. He said he felt Scott's presence with him last night."

"I did too, Mom. I had a beautiful dream. I dreamed Scott was in the room with me, and he was real tall, and he was very, very happy. He radiated light all around him. When I woke up, I had the feeling he was so glad to be rid of his sick body."

The next five days flew past without leaving any feathers behind. The coffeepot bubbled as Mary sat at the kitchen table on Thursday morning. She was writing in her journal.

> I got up early to read the mail that came yesterday. There were so many people here I didn't have time to open it. Gretchen and David have been here this week; it has really been a comfort. Peggy makes it all seem better, somehow. The family service people at church have been bringing us our dinner all week. When Aggie called to say they wanted to, I said "yes" just to make her feel better, but it has been a blessing. We have had so much company, I haven't had time to cook. And the mail! Unbelievable. We have checks from people I have never heard of. Over $500 has come in, most of it in small amounts. I have had a dream way down deep to give a carillon to the church in memory of Scott. To have the hymns he sang ringing up and down the streets where he loved to walk would be to have Scott live on, in a beautiful way. Not very many people knew he was dying. He never told anybody. I want people to hear the songs about the Christ Scott loved. Only Jesus could have given him the faith to walk around with that big smile on his face, when he knew he did not have long to live.
>
> The notes people have written all carry the same themes. "I am so glad I knew him," "I feel so blessed for having known Scott," "I have learned so much about living and loving from Scott," "He taught me how to love," "He brought me joy," "He touched all our lives and made them brighter."

Mary read over the letter that had come from Karen, who had gone to Phoenix on Christmas Day.

"When I hung up the phone I thought, 'No, Scott can't be dead.' I heard the words come forcefully in Scott's own voice, 'I have never been more alive.'

"Then Jesus spoke to my heart saying, 'Now Scott's love for me and his praises are continuous and fulfilled. Come to me for comfort. Do not draw inward. I have Scott in my arms and he is filled with joy. He is very dear to my heart. I gave you Scott as a brother for a season. His work is now complete on earth, and with me he can rest.' "

Mary picked up the top envelope from the pile in front of her. Reading the return address, she thought of the fun they had in the summer when she and Scott spent the weekend with the Orwigs, who lived across from Camp Miniwanca every summer. Kay had written, "Both Jim and I felt blessed to have known and enjoyed Scott. Surely he is with the saints now, and at ease with them as he was with this world. Last summer I had the distinct impression he had a foot in both worlds and was enjoying his special time somewhere halfway between heaven and earth." A note from another camp friend echoed the same theme.

Lynn Wermuth, who had met Scott only over the luncheon table at a crowded department store one noon, wrote, "It was such a pleasure to be able to meet Scott and know him briefly. He was such a sweet, appealing young man with a very interesting, perhaps one might even say 'fascinating' quality of 'other worldliness.' That quality of seeming to be from another world, another time, added great emphasis and meaning to Scott's short time on earth."

Mary saw the envelope with the red ink was from Dirk Debbink, in his third year at Annapolis. Dirk wrote, "As we often remark, the Lord's will works in ways strange to us. But it seems this time his will was a little more evident.

"Scott's faith was, and is, a continuing inspiration to all of us, especially those such as myself who need a little shove once in a while. His cheery greetings and beautiful testimonies to God at work in his life will be with me always. It seemed to me that Scott is perhaps the first person I've ever known who was able to complete his work here in life, and to fulfill that which the Lord had planned for him. Amen."

Mary echoed Dirk's "amen" as she opened the next envelope. As she pulled out the embroidered picture, she knew who had sent it. An old friend whose own body was wasting with muscular dystrophy, had embroidered just such a picture for her when her mother died. She read the note folded in the red manila frame: "Dear Friends, it seems presumptuous to try to say anything that you haven't already thought in prayer, so I will let my pricked fingers and many stitches speak of my sympathy and concern. I do want to tell you something of what I value from Scott.

"Several years ago I was going into the clinic for tests, and I was feeling sorry for myself and disgruntled at not being able to get up the steps easily, and on the steps I met you, Mary, and Scott. It was the first time I had seen him since his operation. He greeted me joyfully, inquired after the whole family, and repeated several times that he was so glad to see me.

"That's all. Not much of a story, maybe, but I stood up straighter, went up those steps as if I had lost twenty pounds, and I made up my mind never to give in to self-pity again. I never have. It was a wonderful legacy, and I know that Scott will never have left us as long as there is one person alive to remember his cheery, 'Hi there!' "

Mary wiped her cheeks with the back of her hand. She picked up her pencil and started writing in her journal.

> I dreamed last night that I saw Scott. I didn't see him as much as sense him, but I knew he was lithe and strong and very tall. I felt his joy. I still had the feeling when I awoke. I have it now. It is as if there is a little bright flashlight turned on inside of me. It reminds me of something Scott wrote last spring, it is in here somewhere."

Mary leafed through the notebook until she found what

she sought. Scott had written, "With the feeling of a little
child in complete simpleness and peace, (he covered this
with the word "HIS") I felt I was in the center of a yellow-
golden complete, warm sphere." And then he had drawn
a picture that looked like a walnut shell, radiating light,
with the word "ME" in the center.

Mary looked out the window, past the oak tree bereft of
leaves, to the outline of the stream. The curving depres-
sion, snow-covered, gave no sign of the current still flowing under the ice. Mary thought of the poem that had
taken shape in the nights she had sat alone in the house,
expressive of the feelings that flowed beneath the surface
of her days. She leafed back through the journal until she
found it. She read it over with a feeling of completion, a
quiet kind of fulfillment, a sense of purpose achieved.

> When did you know he was going away?
> When did you look at your God-Son and say,
> Quietly though, so no one could hear,
> "I did not know that the price was so dear"?

> When you first heard the angels that cold, starry
>   night,
> You did not know they were singing of fright,
> And of pain and of loss and of nails and of blood,
> And of tears welling up in an avalanche flood.

> Where were you, Mom, when he rode on the ass?
> Just one of the crowd who watched him ride past?
> And that night when he knelt in the garden alone,
> Did you lie sleepless, your heart's cry a moan?

> You knew, did you not, he was going away?
> No particular time, not the hour, not the day,
> But that sometime you'd wake up and he would be
>   gone,
> You'd not see his head far away in the throng.

> If you were right here, Mary, what would you say,
> To help ease my grief today?

Would you speak a mystery, "From pain of death,
  new life bursts free"?
From desert hunger's albatross, your son speaks to
  my sense of loss.

In mystic truth, the cross lives on,
Its work complete, yet still not done.
Its blood-stained beams cry out to me,
The peace within my agony.

A Kingdom's coming, here on earth.
We feel the pain, we share the birth.
We live our own Gethsemane.
I kneel with him, he prays through me.

Grief's shapeless mass, dark of my night,
Fuel for his flame, match for his light.
His candlestick He'd have me hold,
The candles burning, blazing gold.

His Spirit hovers over me,
With beating wings, to set me free.

The hot summer sun filtered through the windows of
the basement room where Mary sat at what had been
Scott's desk, filing papers in an accordion pleated paper
folder. She scanned quickly the report labeled "Necropsy
No. 38, 940" which had come in the mail from Massachusetts General Hospital the day before. She read more
carefully the key sentence: "There is no evidence whatever
for recurrent tumor in this case, nor is there any evidence
of Huntington's chorea." Though the doctors were unsure
of the cause of Scott's death, they knew what did not cause
it.

The medical facts skimmed her mind, like a flat stone
skipping across a quiet pond. She tucked the autopsy report away in the file, then picked up the next paper on the
pile on the desk. Her eyes filled with tears as she read the
penciled words Josh had handed to her, wordlessly, the
day after Scott's death.

SONG OF SCOTT

Sing a gentle breeze.
  With first breath of morning,
    sing a gentle breeze.

Life was hard.
  Now my delight is to bless children,
    stir the leaves.

You have questions, and all that is between.
  The Lord shall hold them,
    a fragile moth,
      cupped in his hands,
        then released to fly in peace.

Come with me to the mountaintop.
  Kneel, we'll pray for cities below.
    With the last sigh of dusk we'll
      sing a gentle breeze.